What others are saying...

Throughout history, God, in His grace, has reminded us of the need to proclaim His principles, not as locks by which people need to be restricted, but as keys that set people at liberty. From the early church fathers to the reformers to the burning and shining lights of the 21st century, God has always had some who refuse to accept the religious status quo but instead press forward with an understanding of spiritual things that provokes us to be more like Him. Larry Huch is such a man. His understanding of God's law from the unique historical perspective of God's chosen people will set you at liberty to become more like the One whose face we earnestly seek, whose glory we will see, and at whose feet we will humbly bow in worship.

—Rod Parsley
World Harvest Church, Columbus, OH
Host of television show *Breakthrough*

"*The Torah Blessing* by Pastor Larry Huch is a rich spiritual gold mine of nuggets all Christians should read. Believers will learn the depth of our relationship with our Jewish roots and its importance as it relates to our faith."

—Marcus D. Lamb
President & CEO, Daystar Television Network

"As an orthodox rabbi who is also a believer in Yeshua and pastor of a messianic congregation in Jerusalem, I must say that I am very happy to be associated with Pastor Huch and his congregation. I have known him and watched him for years as his soul and heart have become knit together with the Jewish people and the land of Israel. He has an insatiable hunger and passion to study the Bible and dig out the hidden truths to bring God's revelations to the world. He has continued diligently on this path of study for many years and has had a profound effect on the world with his teachings connecting the New Testament to its Jewish roots. Pastor Larry has a unique gift in that he is able to take deep, ancient biblical truths and teach them in a way that is relevant and life changing. He is able to present these truths in a way that celebrates what the Lord has done in the past and also what He intends to do in the future. He has brought to light mysteries that have been misunderstood, misinterpreted, or overlooked for generations. His message is, without doubt, an end-time revelation and truly *for such a time as this*!"

—Rabbi Joseph Shulam
Director, Netivyah Bible Instruction Ministry, Jerusalem

The Torah BLESSING

Revealing the Mystery,
Releasing the Miracle

LARRY HUCH

WHITAKER
HOUSE

THE TORAH BLESSING:
REVEALING THE MYSTERY, RELEASING THE MIRACLE
revised and expanded

Larry Huch Ministries
P.O. Box 610890
Dallas, TX 75261
phone: 972.313.7133
www.LarryHuchMinistries.com / www.newbeginnings.org

ISBN: 978-1-60374-118-7
Printed in the United States of America
© 2009 by Larry Huch

Whitaker House
1030 Hunt Valley Circle
New Kensington, PA 15068
www.whitakerhouse.com

Library of Congress Cataloging-in-Publication Data

Huch, Larry.
The Torah blessing / by Larry Huch.
   p. cm.
Summary: "Explores the Jewish roots of the Christian faith, explains the implications of being grafted into the covenant promises and inheritance of Israel, and advocates an observation of Torah aspects in order to reach a deeper level of intimacy with our Jewish Messiah"—Provided by publisher.
ISBN 978-1-60374-118-7 (trade pbk. : alk. paper) 1. Messianic Judaism. 2. Jewish Christians—History. 3. Judaism (Christian theology) 4. Christianity—Origin. 5. Christianity and other religions—Judaism. 6. Judaism—Relations—Christianty. I. Title.

BR195.J8H83 2009
289.9—dc22
            2009015232

4 5 6 7 8 9 10 11 12 **LLJ** 16 15 14 13 12 11 10

Dedication

I dedicate this book to my children and their spouses, who have always shared our passion for God, His Word, His people, and our ministry. I'm so proud of each one of you—as a wonderful person and as an integral part of our ministry team. Anna and Brandin (spouse), Luke and Jen (spouse), and Katie...you validate my purpose, and you fill my life with love and fun!

To my "grandsugars," Asher, Judah, and Aviva Shalom, the light and joy of my life.

And, as always, to my wife, Tiz, who, for more than thirty-three years, has brought continual inspiration, support, and love to everything I do.

Foreword

ncient Jewish wisdom teaches that everything God created has its purpose. The great King David wondered about the purpose of a spider until one spun a web over the entrance to a cave in which he was hiding. The pursuing soldiers didn't bother to enter the cave, as they regarded the spiderweb as sufficient indication that David hadn't gone into that cave. That spider saved the Jewish king's life.

For me, the purpose of a spider was more mundane but nonetheless quite thrilling. For years, I had been baffled by a beautiful, large spiderweb that could be seen outside my front door on many a morning. On one side, it was anchored to the wall of my house and the gutter beneath the roof. On the other side, it was attached to a pole. The engineering problem perplexed me. Assuming the spider began her work on the wall of my house, how did she get to the pole four feet away? Did she attach a thread to the wall, then laboriously descend the wall, cross the four feet of concrete to the base of the pole, and ascend the pole all the way, dragging a long thread behind her? Did she then reel in the thread until it was taut and attach it to the pole? That seemed quite impossible, but if that had not been the way, what had been?

I finally found out when I watched the spider clinging to the wall of my house. Her spinnerets pumped out the thinnest, finest thread imaginable. This wafted in the imperceptible air currents for a while before finally drooping down, missing the pole, and dangling uselessly from her body. She severed that thread and made another attempt. Another miss. On the third try, the thread wafted across and grazed against the pole. It was sticky enough to adhere to the surface. Immediately, the spider scuttled across her new "bridge" and began construction of the beautiful web I would later see reflecting the light of the rising sun.

This spider's purpose taught me that the only way to achieve is to produce and project, sometimes without knowing if or where our work will find anchorage.

My friend, Pastor Larry Huch, has known this for quite some time. He has known that his life mission is to inspire, teach, and lead by teaching about our faith's Hebrew origins. He started before it became popular. He projected his powerful innovations, which often wafted around and drooped into obscurity. He did it again and again and again. He never wavered in his determination and never tired of teaching. Finally, after relentless effort, the thread was tethered, and his followers began to multiply. He did what he knew he had to do, whether or not it made him popular, and the sheer vitality, energy, and authenticity of his enterprise brought great blessing to him, his family, and his entire congregation. With this volume in your possession, you will begin to capture some of his excitement. You will be overtaken by an increasingly compelling impulse to know more about Judaism and Hebrew heritage. Pieces will fall into place, mysteries will be resolved, and your faith will be strengthened.

You might wonder how I, an Orthodox Jewish rabbi, who doesn't know very much about Christianity, can assure you that this book will enhance your relationship with God. I respond by pointing out that of the twenty worst natural disasters of the twentieth century, those that resulted in the greatest losses of human life, only three occurred in Christian countries. Now, this certainly is not meant to imply that God hates non-Christian countries and brings natural disasters to afflict them. Note that I did not stipulate the twenty most powerful natural disasters but only those that caused the greatest losses of life. In fact, the April 1991 cyclone that struck Bangladesh was of a slightly lower magnitude than Hurricane Hugo, which battered the Atlantic coast of the United States in the fall of 1989. Hurricane Hugo killed fewer than forty Americans, including some hospital patients. However, the Bangladesh storm two years later killed over 138,000 Bangladeshis. How do we account for this disproportionate loss of life from weather storms of similar magnitudes? The answer is that in Christian countries, the importance of life is a paramount cultural imperative; therefore, they construct seawalls, develop warning systems, and prepare evacuation routes.

In 1953, nearly two thousand Dutchmen drowned when the North Sea breached a dike and flooded part of low-lying Holland. Within a few years, those Protestants had commenced the world's largest civil engineering project, and, though afflicted with the same horrible North Sea weather, Holland has never flooded significantly since. On the other hand, year after year, storms bring floods to many Asian countries in which people die by the tens of thousands. No warning systems exist, let alone seawalls or evacuation routes.

And it is not only flooding. On December 23, 2003, a massive earthquake registering 6.5 on the Richter scale struck central California around the town of Paso Robles. Only two people were killed. Three days later, on December 26, 2003, over thirty-thousand victims perished in an Iranian earthquake in the town of Bam. To explain the vast death toll inflicted by an earthquake no stronger than the one that had struck Paso Robles, Iranian authorities pleaded poverty. The truth is that it costs considerably more to engineer large-scale nuclear facilities, as Iran has done, than it costs to retrofit buildings for safety in an earthquake-prone zone. The problem is not poverty; it is priority.

Here in the United States, a primary standard-bearer of Christian civilization, we have two cultural imperatives imbedded deeply within our national DNA. Both flow from the Bible, with which our country's founders were intimately familiar, and by means of which they sculpted their worldviews.

Our first distinctive cultural imperative is to render ourselves less vulnerable to nature. We believed we were following divine will when we developed medicine and medical technology to dominate disease. We found insecticides to protect our food supply. We built dams to protect populations from flooding rivers. We took seriously the commandment in Genesis 1:28, when God told Adam and Eve, *"Be fruitful and multiply; fill the earth and subdue it."* We never understood *"subdue it"* to mean obliterating nature or otherwise despoiling the environment. We knew it involved practicing responsible stewardship and making ourselves less vulnerable to nature, which is not always benign. We knew we were pleasing God by making ourselves safer and more secure, and this knowledge lent urgency and meaning to our efforts, which then seemed to be blessed. Not by coincidence did the overwhelming majority of these scientific and technical developments take place in the West.

Western civilization's second distinctive cultural imperative is the importance of preserving human life. This, too, derives directly from our biblical roots and distinguishes us from the peculiar fatalism toward death found in so many other cultures.

Together, these two biblical values enshrined in the West, in general—and in America, in particular—are chiefly responsible for the vastly diminished impact that natural disasters have inflicted upon Western society.

In other words, it is clear to me that ancient Jewish wisdom enshrined in the Bible can banish barbarism and cultivate civilization. It creates more successful cultures, societies, and countries. In the same way, I believe that the ancient Jewish wisdom enshrined in the Bible, which my friend Pastor Larry Huch reveres and teaches, can bring transformation to your life and a sense of awe to your faith.

I am thrilled that God led him to write this book, and I wish him a *Mazal tov*—great good fortune. May your adventures in spiritual growth be rewarded by your excursion through this volume.

—Rabbi Daniel Lapin
The American Alliance of Jews and Christians
Mercer Island, Washington

Contents

Introduction: My Journey of No Return 13

1. Our Family Tree 19

2. Building a Temple 29

3. Grace and the Law: The Arrow That Points to Jesus 41

4. The Missing Piece to a 2000-Year-Old Puzzle:
   Tearing Down the Wall 59

5. The Tallit (Prayer Shawl): Healing in His Wings 87

6. The Sabbath: Our Appointed Time 99

7. What Would Jesus Do?: First, He'd Admit That He's a Jew 115

8. A Shabbat for All People 125

The Seven Feasts 141

9. The Feasts of Passover, Unleavened Bread, and Firstfruits 145

10. The Feast of Pentecost 171

11. The Feast of Rosh Hashanah (New Year) 177

12. The Feast of Yom Kippur (Day of Atonement) 187

13. The Feast of Sukkot (Tabernacles) 201

14. Your Exciting Journey 207

Appendix: The Seven Major Jewish Feasts 211

Glossary of Terms 213

About the Author 217

Introduction:
My Journey of No Return

Thirteen years ago, I found myself on my very first trip to Israel. It was not a trip I had been dying to make. After all, as a Christian, I had been taught that God was essentially done with Israel and that the Jews had received their chance to accept Jesus as Messiah but had blown it. I was taught that the "church"—not a denomination or building, but the believers who formed the body of Christ—had replaced Israel; in fact, the church *was* Israel.

I was so misguided. *Nothing* could have been further from the truth.

I certainly wasn't looking to "reconnect with my Jewish roots" on this trip. I wouldn't even have known what that phrase meant. I was, however, dealing with a gnawing feeling that, as a pastor, I dared not utter in the light of day: there was something missing in my life and in my Christian faith.

Have you ever felt like that? In your quiet, solitary moments, have you ever wondered or even prayed,

God, what's wrong?
I love You; I'm serving You; I believe Your Word.
I know that You are the same yesterday, today, and forever. I know it's all true.
So why does it feel like something is missing in my life?

If you've ever struggled with those thoughts, you're not alone. I know exactly what you're going through. It was with this mind-set that I embarked on my trip to Israel.

After I arrived in the Holy Land, one of the first places my Israeli friends took me was Capernaum. Despite my hesitancy, I was truly excited to go there because I knew this to be the location of one of the great stories of the Bible. Capernaum was the place where Jesus healed Peter's mother-in-law, described in Mark 1:29–39.

As we walked through the gates, the remains of Peter's house were directly ahead of us. It's one of the most popular tourist attractions in all of Israel. Many people who go there, however, miss another spot of equal importance. Turn to your right after passing through the gates, and you will see the remains of an ancient synagogue. Joseph, my friend from Jerusalem, began to tell me all about this holy place of Jewish worship. As he did so, I couldn't help but think, *So what? What does this synagogue have to do with me? I'm a believer in Jesus.* Then, Joseph pointed out an inscription on the doorpost. It indicated that the synagogue had been dedicated by the grandchildren of the apostles of Jesus. As the group began to walk away, I remained transfixed. I stopped the group and said, "Joseph, tell me again who dedicated this synagogue."

He told me again.

"How can that be?" I asked. "Weren't the descendants of the apostles Christians? Weren't they followers of Jesus?"

Joseph said, "Of course, they were."

Still confused, I asked, "Then what would a believer in Jesus be doing in a synagogue? Did they backslide?"

The next few words changed my life, and I believe they will change yours, too. It was the reason God had brought me to Israel. It was the answer I had been looking for.

"Larry," he said, "the church and the synagogue were synonymous for three hundred and twenty-five years after Christ's resurrection. Jesus never intended for His followers to be separated from Israel, from God's people, or from the Torah. As Christians, we were to be *grafted* in."

As Joseph led the rest of the group to Peter's house, I remained. I wasn't alone, though, for my God—the God of Israel, the God of the Jews, the God of that synagogue—was right there with me. He gently said to me, "Larry, I'm going to open your eyes. I'm going to teach you how to read My Word, not with the eyes of a Gentile Jesus, not with the eyes of a Protestant Jesus or a Catholic Jesus, but with the eyes of a Jewish Jesus. I'm going to show you what you've been missing."

Standing at the entrance of a two-thousand-year-old synagogue in Capernaum, Israel, on the Sea of Galilee, I was stunned by a profound revelation: Jesus was a Jew—a practicing, observant Jew. Not only that, but His disciples and followers were also practicing Jews.

For some, this may seem like a "no brainer," but for me, in that moment, I was struck with a revelation that completely altered my understanding of who Jesus was—and therefore who *I* was as a Christian. The inscription on that synagogue was a dedication by the Christian descendants of Jesus' disciples. For generations, followers of Jesus had continued to attend synagogue, maintaining their observance of the Jewish faith and lifestyle.

That experience led me to see Jesus and the entire Bible in a fresh, new light. It was a paradigm shift—a total uprooting of how I had been taught to read the Word of God and how I had followed Jesus. As a result, it was a total shift in how I saw myself and lived my life as a Christian.

The journey I've since taken to uncover and understand the Jewish roots of my Christian faith has been, aside from the moment of my salvation, the most transformative, exciting, and fulfilling experience of my life. I began to read Scripture from a Jewish perspective rather than from the Greek- or Roman-influenced doctrine I had been taught as a young believer. I realized that Jesus and His disciples weren't *converted* Jews but rather were *practicing* Jews—keepers of the Torah. I began to understand that, for a follower of Jesus, there is profound power and revelation in understanding the Torah—not only by studying it, but also by keeping and sharing in many of its customs and celebrations.

I was hooked. I can't emphasize enough the impact this revelation has had on my life. The more I investigated, the more I began to experience an incredible fullness in my life as a Christian. The "Jewishness" of my

Messiah was the missing piece that opened up an entirely new revelation of God's Word. The Bible began to come alive in a way I had never experienced but had always sought. I was now reading the Bible and Jesus' teachings from the perspective with which they had been written. It has brought fulfillment not only in my spiritual life, but also in my family, ministry, finances, and every single aspect of my life. It has led me to become a better person by truly understanding what it means to be *"the light of the world"* (Matthew 5:14).

It has been my experience that without prior introduction to the idea of Jewish roots being essential to Christianity, many believers are hesitant to open their hearts and minds to what it truly means. Perhaps they fear that by doing so they would be setting aside all that Jesus has done for them. As you'll soon learn, that couldn't be further from the truth. The true understanding of who Jesus was as a Jew makes everything He did for us all the more powerful and meaningful. His teachings and the way He lived and died will begin to come alive in ways that you've never known.

The vast majority of responses I continue to get from thousands of people who have received this teaching is that the revelation and truth "just clicked." That may sound too simple, but it's true. I can't say it any better than that. There's something about reading the Word of God through this new yet original light that feels so right. It just "clicks" in your spirit. I believe this will be your experience, too.

What hit me like a lightning bolt over a decade ago has led to a revolution. We're now seeing people around the world who are desperately hungry for knowledge of their Jewish roots, as well as for the wisdom and revelation of the Torah. There is a growing recognition that we, as Christians, are not, and never were meant to be, separated from or foreigners to our Jewish roots. On the contrary, we are to be *grafted in*, connected to the roots. We are fellow branches of the same tree.

Wouldn't you like to see the promises of God's Word come alive in every area of your life through the Holy Spirit? What if I could show you that God's anointing for your family, your finances, and your future has always been right in front of you, but the enemy has blurred your eyes until now? The season of harvest for God's blessings is now, in every area of your life.

If, like so many others, you have been hungry for the truth—truth that will set you free—then won't you come with me on the journey of a lifetime?

My prayer is that, as you read this book, you will experience a paradigm shift as I did on that day in Capernaum. As you uncover the Jewish roots of your Christian faith, I pray that it will reveal the mysteries of God's Word and release His mighty miracles—*The Torah Blessing*—into every area of your life.

May God bless you,
Larry Huch

1

Our Family Tree

e hear this Scripture quoted all the time: "*The truth shall make you free.*" Allow me to let you in on a little secret: it's *not* true. I know many of you are shocked right now. You may be thinking, *How can Pastor Larry say that? It's in the Bible. Jesus Himself said it. I've heard it taught time and time again: "The truth shall make you free."*

I'm here to tell you, "No, it will not." Why? It won't because that's not what the Bible says. Let's look at this passage together:

> *Then Jesus said to those Jews who believed Him, "If you abide in My word, you are My disciples indeed. And you shall know the truth, and the truth shall make you free."*   (John 8:31–32)

Once again, some of you are now thinking, *Don't you see, Pastor Larry? It's right there in front of you: "The truth shall make you free."* But is that really what Jesus was saying? Look again at verse 32. Do you see it? Jesus first said, "*And you shall know the truth.*" This means that you will understand the truth; then, and only then—when you know God's Word *and* you understand God's Word—will that truth "*make you free.*" Once we understand God's concepts, they have the power to set us free. If we remain ignorant of what the Bible says, it remains the truth, but that truth won't do us much good until we understand it. Let me give you some examples.

Before I met Jesus, I was a drug dealer and an addict. The *truth* was that Jesus came two thousand years ago to forgive me, change me, and love me, but the miracle-working *power* of that truth did me no good until somebody told me about it so I could fully *understand* it. The truths that Jesus died on the cross, that He rose again on the third day, that He was

> **So many promises of God never come alive for us because we don't fully *know* and *understand* them.**

the Lamb of God who took away my sins, and that He came to set the captives free were real, but they did not set me free until I *knew* them. Once I accepted Jesus Christ as my Savior and began to understand those truths, the Word of God jumped off the pages of the Bible and changed from *logos* (the Greek word for written words on a page) to *rhema* (the Greek word for God's Word, alive and working in my spirit). Just as Jesus was the Word of God become flesh, *rhema* is the truth of God's Word made alive for you and me. So many promises of God never come alive for us, His children, because we don't fully *know* and *understand* them.

Water Closets and Hogs

Unfortunately, one of the main reasons people fail to understand truth has to do with the many differences and complexities of language. Years ago, Tiz and I moved to Australia to pastor our second church. Soon after moving there, we were visiting a pastor's home, and before we sat down to eat, I asked him, "May I use your bathroom?" He pointed down the hall and said, "Second door on the right." I followed his directions, and, sure enough, there was a sink, a tub, and a shower, but, unfortunately for me, not the item I really needed to use. After a few minutes of frustration, I came out with embarrassment and admitted, "I'm sorry, but I can't find it."

He asked, "What are you looking for?"

I shared my biological need with him, and he said, "Oh, you're not looking for the bathroom; you're looking for the water closet!"

On that day, I learned an important lesson: in Australia, the "water closet" is the toilet and the "bathroom" is literally the room in which you take a bath. Once I understood that truth, it became very useful to me.

Here's another example. Let's say I hand you my wallet and ask, "Would you mind putting this wallet in my *boot*?" How would you interpret that? If you were from Texas, you'd probably put my wallet into my Tony Llama cowboy footwear. On the other hand, if you were from South Africa, you would most likely toss it into the trunk of my car. The same word is used—even the same spelling—but two totally different meanings are inferred.

You don't have to be from the other side of the globe to find this kind of confusion. If somebody told you, "Pastor Larry was seen riding a thousand-pound *hog,*" what would that mean to you? If you were from Arkansas—the Razorback State—you might picture me saddled on the back of a very large animal with a snout. If, however, you were from south St. Louis, like I am, you would probably picture me riding around on a thousand-pound Harley Davidson motorcycle—which would be the truth. Again, the same word is used, but the interpretation is different depending on your upbringing, experience, and culture—and this is for people who live in the same time period! Imagine the difficulties that occur when you introduce different languages, cultures, and a two-thousand-year or more separation of time.

To glean all of God's truth from Scripture, we need to learn to read the Bible not merely from a twenty-first century American or European perspective but also from the perspective of the times and cultures in which it was written—particularly, the Jewish world of first-century Jerusalem and surrounding Israel. Those who wrote the Bible may have spoken Hebrew, Greek, Latin, and Aramaic, but, for the most part, they thought and reasoned with Jewish mind-sets.

No Longer Gentiles, No Longer Strangers

Let us begin by focusing on an important passage of Scripture. Even though it was written more than two thousand years ago, I believe it remains a prophetic word for us today.

Therefore remember that you, once Gentiles in the flesh; who are called Uncircumcision by what is called the Circumcision made in the flesh by hands; that at that time you were without Christ, being aliens from the commonwealth of Israel and strangers from the covenants of promise, having no hope and without God in the world. But now in Christ Jesus you who once were far off have been brought near by the blood of Christ. For He Himself is our peace, who has made both one, and has broken down the middle wall of separation, having abolished in His flesh the enmity, that is, the law of commandments contained in ordinances, so as to create in Himself one new man from the two, thus making peace, and that He might reconcile them both to God in one body through the cross, thereby putting to death the enmity. And He came and preached peace to you who were afar off and to those who were near. For through Him we both have access by one Spirit to the Father. Now, therefore, you are no longer strangers and foreigners, but fellow citizens with the saints and members of the household of God, having been built on the foundation of the apostles and prophets, Jesus Christ Himself being the chief corner stone, in whom the whole building, being joined together, grows into a holy temple in the Lord, in whom you also are being built together for a dwelling place of God in the Spirit.

(Ephesians 2:11–22)

I know that this is a long passage of Scripture, but let's take a moment to break down these powerful words.

Paul said we were *"once Gentiles."* This is very important. If you are not of Jewish blood but have asked Jesus Christ to come into your heart and forgive you of your sins, you were *once* a Gentile, but not anymore! *Gentile* in Greek is the word *ethnos*, defined by *Strong's Exhaustive Concordance* as "foreign nations not worshipping the true God, pagans." In addition to the word *Gentile*, the Bible also uses words such as *foreigners*, *strangers*, and *nations*—all referring to those who do not worship the one true God, the God of Israel, the God of Abraham, Isaac, and Jacob; the God who sent His Son, Jesus, to pay the price for our sins in full so that we could go boldly before Him.

Look at what it says later in this passage: *"Now, therefore, you are no longer strangers and foreigners, but fellow citizens with the saints and members of the household of God"* (verse 19). Paul was referring to us. We were *once* strangers, but *now* we are fellow citizens with the saints—the church—and members of the household of God with Israel.

Redeemed and Reconnected

As a Christian, you have probably heard time and time again that you have been "redeemed by the blood of Jesus." When we become believers, we are restored as children of the covenant promises of God through the shed blood of Jesus. Here are just a couple of examples from Scripture:

> *Knowing that you were not redeemed with corruptible things, like sil-*
> *ver or gold, from your aimless conduct received by tradition from your*
> *fathers, but with the precious blood of Christ.*   (1 Peter 1:18–19)

> *You are worthy to take the scroll, and to open its seals; for You were*
> *slain, and have redeemed us to God by Your blood out of every tribe*
> *and tongue and people and nation.*   (Revelation 5:9)

Ephesians 2 makes it clear that without Jesus, we were aliens, strangers, and foreigners—disconnected from God. Now, thanks to our redemption, God has reconnected us to two very important things.

1. We Have Been Adopted into a New Family

First, we are now part of the family of Israel. The apostle Paul had a unique way of explaining this for a first-century audience who was familiar with growing things from the earth:

> *If some of the branches were broken off, and you, being a wild olive tree,*
> *were **grafted in** among them, and with them became a partaker of the*
> *root and fatness of the olive tree, do not boast against the branches. But*
> *if you do boast, remember that you do not support the root, but the root*
> *supports you.*   (Romans 11:17–18, emphasis added)

This is such an important passage for our study that we will be returning to it several more times. For now, however, I want you to see that you and I—non-Jewish Christians—have been *"grafted in"* to the tree. The branches of that tree are Israel. According to Scripture, we have been adopted—*grafted*—into the family of Israel by the life and blood of Jesus Christ. Our faith, therefore, is not isolated; it does not exist independently, and it is not to be treated as a "spin-off" religion. We are not spiritual orphans. We belong to a living, spiritual "family tree" that is supported by a common root—Jesus Christ, the Messiah. *"Remember that you do not support the root, but the root supports you."* The Bible makes this clear in both the Old and New Testaments:

In that day there shall be a Root of Jesse, who shall stand as a banner to the people; for the Gentiles shall seek Him, and His resting place shall be glorious. (Isaiah 11:10)

I, Jesus, have sent My angel to testify to you these things in the churches. I am the Root and the Offspring of David, the Bright and Morning Star. (Revelation 22:16)

2. We Are Legal Heirs of Abraham's Covenant

Second, now that we have been adopted into the family, we are also connected to the promise God made to His children—His covenant promise.

Therefore know that only those who are of faith are sons of Abraham. And the Scripture, foreseeing that God would justify the Gentiles by faith, preached the gospel to Abraham beforehand, saying, "In you all the nations shall be blessed." So then those who are of faith are blessed with believing Abraham. (Galatians 3:7–9)

Like any child who is adopted into a family, we now have equal rights as legal heirs within that family. In this case, our adoption is all thanks to the shed blood of Jesus. We are now children of the covenant. What covenant? God's covenant with Abraham, who at the time was known as Abram:

Now the LORD had said to Abram: "Get out of your country, from your family and from your father's house, to a land that I will show you. I will make you a great nation; I will bless you and make your name great; and you shall be a blessing. I will bless those who bless you, and I will curse him who curses you; and in you all the families of the earth shall be blessed." (Genesis 12:1–3)

With that, Abram became the first Hebrew. Notice I didn't say Israelite, because at this time, obviously, there was no land of Israel. You might say he became the first Jewish person on the face of the earth. How did this come about?

According to Jewish tradition, Abram grew up working in his father's shop, which sold idols, although he always questioned his father's beliefs.

One day, according to the teaching, young Abram smashed all the idols with a hammer while his father was away and then placed the hammer by one spared idol. When his father returned, Abram blamed the crime on that idol. His father grew upset and claimed that the story was impossible since these idols had no life or power. Abram agreed and asked, "Then why do you worship them?" The teaching suggests that Abram believed the universe to be the work of a single creator and began to share this with others. Of course, this account is from the Jewish Midrash—oral Torah teachings—and not our Scriptures, but the Old Testament does agree that Abram's family worshipped idols. (See Joshua 24:2.)

> **Young Abram's faith in one true God was the seed that would become Israel.**

However it happened, young Abram's faith in one true God was the seed that would become Israel—the children of God. Later, God would say to the nation of Israel,

> *Listen to Me, you who follow after righteousness, you who seek the LORD: look to the rock from which you were hewn, and to the hole of the pit from which you were dug. Look to Abraham your father, and to Sarah who bore you; for I called him alone, and blessed him and increased him.* (Isaiah 51:1–2)

Now, some of you may be thinking, *But Pastor Larry, when God said, "Look to Abraham your father," wasn't He talking to Israel and not to us?*

It's true that He was addressing Israel, but it is also true that you and I have been "grafted in." Let me ask you a question: Are you Christ's? If your answer is yes, then God says that you are Abraham's seed. It doesn't matter if you were born in Africa, Europe, Asia, Australia, North America, South America, or Antarctica—if you are a non-Jewish Christian, you were *once* a Gentile, but now that you've been born again, you are no longer a stranger but the seed of Abraham and an heir, according to the promise.

The Olive Tree

In Romans 11, the apostle Paul compares Israel to an olive tree. Now that we understand that the tree we've been grafted into is Israel, let's look at some biblical and historical features of the olive tree. Throughout this book, I will be referring to the fact that everything God teaches us has both a *physical* side and a *spiritual* side, an *earthly* side and a *heavenly* side. When we look at the features of a *physical* olive tree, we can see the same blessings on the *spiritual* olive tree, Israel.

1. Olive trees outlive most other fruit trees. Likewise, Israel and the Jewish people have outlived all the empires that have enslaved them or tried to destroy them, including the Persian empire, the Babylonian empire, the Ottoman empire, and the Roman empire. They even outlived the Nazi government, the "Thousand Year Reich," that attempted to annihilate them.

   "No weapon formed against you shall prosper, and every tongue which rises against you in judgment you shall condemn. This is the heritage of the servants of the LORD, and their righteousness is from Me," says the LORD. (Isaiah 54:17)

2. The roots of an olive tree are strong and are able to live in all soils. Likewise, throughout history, even though the Jewish people have been scattered about the world among different races and cultures, Judaism has survived and remained intact.

   Thus says the LORD, who created you, O Jacob, and He who formed you, O Israel: "Fear not, for I have redeemed you; I have called you by your name; you are Mine. When you pass through the waters, I will be with you; and through the rivers, they shall not overflow you. When you walk through the fire, you shall not be burned, nor shall the flame scorch you." (Isaiah 43:1–2)

3. Even in very old olive trees, shoots are able to spring up and reproduce. Despite persecution and dispersement, Judaism has grown and the population of Israel has increased.

   Your wife shall be like a fruitful vine in the very heart of your house, your children like olive plants all around your table. (Psalm 128:3)

4. Even today, olive oil remains a major source of wealth. Likewise, God has continually blessed Israel with provision whenever its people have needed it.

Therefore you shall keep the commandments of the LORD your God, to walk in His ways and to fear Him. For the LORD your God is bringing you into a good land, a land of brooks of water, of fountains and springs, that flow out of valleys and hills; a land of wheat and barley, of vines and fig trees and pomegranates, a land of olive oil and honey; a land in which you will eat bread without scarcity, in which you will lack nothing; a land whose stones are iron and out of whose hills you can dig copper....And you shall remember the LORD your God, for it is He who gives you power to get wealth, that He may establish His covenant which He swore to your fathers, as it is this day.

(Deuteronomy 8:6–9, 18)

5. Olive oil is used as both fuel and food. Likewise, throughout history, Judaism has both sustained and provided for its people.

As the living Father sent Me, and I live because of the Father, so he who feeds on Me will live because of Me. (John 6:57)

6. Olive oil is used for anointing and healing. The calling of God to His people is the same: be set apart as a blessing to others.

You shall make from these a holy anointing oil, an ointment compounded according to the art of the perfumer. It shall be a holy anointing oil....And you shall speak to the children of Israel, saying: "This shall be a holy anointing oil to Me throughout your generations."

(Exodus 30:25, 31)

So [the apostles] went out and preached that people should repent. And they cast out many demons, and anointed with oil many who were sick, and healed them. (Mark 6:12–13)

It quickly becomes obvious—and exciting—why it is such a blessing to be grafted into the promises and covenant of Israel—God's olive tree. Remember what God says, throughout the Bible, about Israel and the Jewish people:

1.) They are the apple of God's eye—always have been, always will be.

Thus says the LORD of hosts: "He sent Me after glory, to the nations which plunder you; for he who touches you, touches the apple of His eye." (Zechariah 2:8)

2.) They are a people chosen to be a blessing to the rest of the world.

The Jewish people, and their Promised Land of Israel, were chosen to connect the rest of the world to the God of Abraham, Isaac, and Jacob. God said,

I will make you a great nation; I will bless you and make your name great; and you shall be a blessing. I will bless those who bless you, and I will curse him who curses you; and in you all the families of the earth shall be blessed. (Genesis 12:2–3)

Now that we know our heritage—our spiritual family tree—we can begin to focus on what this means for our lives and our faith, and we can learn how our blended, sometimes dysfunctional family is supposed to live together.

It's simple. We need to build the right kind of house.

2

Building a Temple

Often, when I'm traveling and teaching in a new place, I will ask the audience a question: How many of you believe that God's Word, the Bible, is, without exception, the most powerful thing in the world? The crowd will usually shout out an enthusiastic "Amen!" or "You bet!" You should see the looks on their faces when I tell them that they're wrong. I do all this for effect, but it also makes an important point. Obviously, I strongly affirm that the Bible is the infallible Word of God. But what about those beliefs we embrace that don't come from God but from man's religions or traditions?

Jesus often faced this when He went up against the empty religious actions and motives of the Pharisees. When He addressed the very "religious," Jesus pulled no punches:

Well did Isaiah prophesy of you hypocrites, as it is written: "This people honors Me with their lips, but their heart is far from Me. And in vain they worship Me, teaching as doctrines the commandments of men." For laying aside the commandment of God, you hold the tradition of men. (Mark 7:6–8)

Then, He unloaded the hard truth that they were *"**making the word of God of no effect** through your tradition which you have handed down"* (verse 13, emphasis added). Jesus seemed to be implying that there are man-made traditions passed down through generations that can cause God's Word to become *"of no effect"*—completely devoid of power.

As we continue on this journey together, we will be pulling back the curtains of tradition that have been hung by generations of religious and denominational teachings. As we do, I want us to go beyond the traditions of man and into the truth of God's Word. When we do, as Jesus has taught us, the truth you *know*, the truth you *understand*, shall make you free.

Faith Plus Knowledge

God says that His people—those who know Him, love Him, and follow Him—will be destroyed for one reason and one reason only: a lack of knowledge.

My people are destroyed for lack of knowledge. Because you have rejected knowledge, I also will reject you from being priest for Me.
(Hosea 4:6)

The apostle Peter also taught us the benefits of adding to our faith a bit of knowledge:

His divine power has given to us all things that pertain to life and godliness, through the knowledge of Him who called us by glory and virtue, by which have been given to us exceedingly great and precious promises, that through these you may be partakers of the divine nature, having escaped the corruption that is in the world through lust. But also for this very reason, giving all diligence, add to your faith virtue, to virtue knowledge. (2 Peter 1:3–5)

On our journey together, God is going to add knowledge to your faith. His desire is for you to know and understand the mysteries of the Bible.

Apostles and Prophets

And He Himself gave some to be apostles, some prophets, some evangelists, and some pastors and teachers, for the equipping of the saints for the work of ministry, for the edifying of the body of Christ, till we all come to the unity of the faith and of the knowledge of the Son of God, to

a perfect man, to the measure of the stature of the fullness of Christ.
(Ephesians 4:11–13)

According to this passage in Ephesians, God has given us apostles, prophets, evangelists, pastors, and teachers in order to explain His Word and equip the saints for the work of ministry. Now look at the next verse. This needs to continue until *"we all come to the unity of the faith and of the knowledge of the Son of God."* We need to have a unity of faith that acknowledges Jesus Christ as the Son of God, Messiah, King of Kings, Lord of Lords, and Savior. To that faith, however, we need to add *"the knowledge of the Son of God."*

In this context, I believe that *faith* refers to our adherence to the New Testament and that *knowledge* refers to our spiritual heritage in the Old Testament. I believe that we need to add to our faith in Jesus Christ a knowledge of the Torah. When that happens, we then become *"a perfect man"*—a mature man or woman of God. Then *"the fullness of Christ"* comes upon us—everything that Jesus paid for by His blood and everything the Word of God promises us.

Don't get me wrong. I'm not saying that there are no instances of faith in the Old Testament. Certainly, when Abraham placed Isaac on the altar as a sacrifice, as God had instructed, he was demonstrating phenomenal faith. (See Genesis 22:1–14.) On the other hand, when Paul reasoned with the men of Athens, he was incorporating knowledge into the gospel message. (See Acts 17:22–32.) Overall, however, I believe there is a great blessing available when we add to our faith in Christ knowledge of the Torah. Then, we are able to experience the true fullness of Christ.

Laying the Foundation

*Therefore, you are no longer strangers and foreigners, but fellow citizens with the saints and members of the household of God, having been built on **the foundation of the apostles and prophets**, Jesus Christ Himself being the chief corner stone, in whom the whole building, being joined together, grows into a holy temple in the Lord.*
(Ephesians 2:19–21, emphasis added)

The household of God is built on the foundation of the apostles (whose teachings we call the New Testament) and also on the prophets (what we call the Old Testament)—with Jesus Christ Himself being the chief cornerstone. We're no longer Gentiles because we have been grafted in as members of the family of the God of Abraham, Isaac, and Jacob. We're now members of a household built upon the teachings of the Old Testament and the New Testament. On one side are the prophets, on the other side are the apostles, and Jesus is holding it all together. If we're going to grow *"into a holy temple in the Lord"*—if we are going to see the anointing and power of God—then we've got to build our temple with the foundation of both the New Testament and the Old Testament. We have hope because, through His life and blood, Jesus has connected us to both covenants and to all of God's promises.

> *Therefore know that only those who are of faith are sons of Abraham. And the Scripture, foreseeing that God would justify the Gentiles by faith, preached the gospel to Abraham beforehand, saying, "In you all the nations shall be blessed."* (Galatians 3:7–8)

Those who are of faith are blessed with the ability to look to Abraham. We who believe in Jesus are the wild branch that has been grafted into the olive tree that is Israel. The roots of that olive tree are the God of Abraham, Isaac, and Jacob, and we who are of faith are now called the sons of Abraham.

One House, One Family, One New Man

> *He Himself is our peace, who has made both one, and has broken down the middle wall of separation, having abolished in His flesh the enmity, that is, the law of commandments contained in ordinances, so as to create in Himself one new man from the two, thus making peace.* (Ephesians 2:14–15)

> *"On that day I will raise up the tabernacle of David, which has fallen down, and repair its damages; I will raise up its ruins, and rebuild it as in the days of old; that they may possess the remnant of Edom, and all the Gentiles who are called by My name," says the LORD who does this thing.* (Amos 9:11–12)

I believe that the key to a great outpouring of God's power is found in these two amazing Scriptures. First, let's look at James' interpretation of the prophecy that God gave to the prophet Amos, as recorded by Luke in the book of Acts:

> *James answered, saying, "...Simon has declared how God at the first visited the Gentiles to take out of them a people for His name. And with this the words of the prophets agree, just as it is written: 'After this I will return and will rebuild the tabernacle of David, which has fallen down; I will rebuild its ruins, and I will set it up; so that the rest of mankind may seek the LORD, even all the Gentiles who are called by My name, says the LORD who does all these things.' Known to God from eternity are all His works."* (Acts 15:13–18)

God's Blended Family

The blending of this family did not come easily to the early church. To more fully understand this, you should take a few moments to read Acts 15:1–21. Your Bible probably labels this portion of Scripture, "The Jerusalem Council." In this passage, the early church was experiencing a twofold problem. First, Gentiles were becoming believers in Jesus Christ. *"And the Lord added to the church daily those who were being saved"* (Acts 2:47). Unfortunately, many of these Gentiles had no idea of how to act now that they were *"no longer Gentiles"* but children of God. They didn't have a clue. Second, some of the leaders of the early church felt that all the Gentiles who were being grafted into the family of God through Jesus Christ had to be circumcised, in keeping with Jewish law.

> *Some of the sect of the Pharisees who believed rose up, saying, "It is necessary to circumcise them, and to command them to keep the law of Moses."* (Acts 15:5)

Here's the Key

Remember, everything God does has both a spiritual side and a physical side. Knowing that, let's look at both the Old and the New

Testaments. The Bible was never meant to be split in half. In fact, God's Word wasn't called the Old Testament and New Testament until the fourth century.

The Bible itself says that the first (Old) Testament was a shadow of good things to come.

> For the law, having a shadow of the good things to come, and not the very image of the things, can never with these same sacrifices, which they offer continually year by year, make those who approach perfect.
> (Hebrews 10:1)

Think about a shadow. As I sit at my desk right now, the light above me is casting the shadow of my hand onto the page I'm writing. The shadow is of my hand—not a different hand or someone else's hand or a fake hand, but *my* hand. In Acts 15:5 they were debating about what to do with those former Gentiles? Should they physically be circumcised in their flesh? Then, they realized that God had already circumcised them, spiritually, in their hearts.

> For "the name of God is blasphemed among the Gentiles because of you," as it is written. (Romans 2:24)

Now, here is the key to you understanding the rest of this book. When you understand what I'm about to say, you'll begin the most exciting journey of your Christian walk! You'll begin to understand what I mean by *The Torah Blessing: Revealing the Mystery, Releasing the Miracle*.

By Grace or By Works?

As Christians, one of the first things we are taught is that there is nothing—I repeat, *nothing*—we can do to *earn* our salvation. On this point, the Bible is crystal clear:

> But God, who is rich in mercy, because of His great love with which He loved us, even when we were dead in trespasses, made us alive together with Christ (by grace you have been saved)....For by grace you have been saved through faith, and that not of yourselves; it is the gift of God, not of works, lest anyone should boast. (Ephesians 2:4–5, 8–9)

And it shall come to pass that whoever calls on the name of the LORD
shall be saved. (Acts 2:21)

*So they said, "Believe on the Lord Jesus Christ, and you will be saved,
you and your household."* (Acts 16:31)

God gave the Jerusalem Council the wisdom to realize that these former
Gentiles had come into the family of God through the grace of Jesus Christ.
As such, they received not only salvation but also the blessing of God's covenant promises, which were paid in full by the blood of the Lamb. It was agreed
that it was now circumcision of the heart, not of the flesh, that saved through
faith in Jesus Christ. In order to begin worshipping together, therefore, these
new converts needed to begin taking some baby steps of obedience—four
simple things. Today, they almost sound ridiculous. Remember, though, that
these former Gentiles knew absolutely *nothing* of the Torah—God's Word.

Things may have seemed confusing when you were first saved, too. That's
how it was for me. The night I received Jesus Christ as my Lord and Savior,
I felt so wonderful that, without knowing any better, I went out and bought
a bag of marijuana to smoke in celebration. That may sound preposterous
to you, but it's true. I knew absolutely *nothing* about what it meant to serve
and follow God. I was much like those Gentile believers in Acts. I had been
completely saved by the grace of God, but I had to be led step-by-step in my
Christian walk. I wouldn't have been able to handle big assignments. My first
step was simply to clean my house of idols—specifically, my drug use.

The early church leaders said, in essence, "Listen, these people are
saved by grace. Let's not load them down with rules. Let's make it simple
to begin with. No idols, okay? No fornication, okay? No more sacrificing
strangled animals, okay? And, oh yeah, no more drinking of blood!" (See
Acts 15:19–21.)

As we grow in our Christian walk, we soon learn that there is much in
God's Word that doesn't *save* us but, as we become obedient, brings great
blessings to our lives. Scripture tells us,

*Children, obey your parents in the Lord, for this is right....that it may
be well with you and you may live long on the earth.*
(Ephesians 6:1, 3)

> **Our obedience to God is not to earn favor or salvation but for our own good.**

In the same way, our obedience to God's ways is not to earn favor or salvation but for our own good. For instance, tithing, or giving back to God financially, doesn't save me, but doing so brings a wealth of blessing that goes far beyond anything I am able to give Him.

The first church knew this, too. The Torah, the law of Moses, was being taught in all the synagogues on every Sabbath. These former Gentiles who were now grafted into the olive tree—Israel—were going to be in the synagogue every Sabbath. They would grow in their knowledge of God as they heard the Torah being read. Just like new Christians today, as God's Word began to enter their hearts, they soon found themselves better able to reap the benefits and blessings of obedience.

No Wall of Separation

Here, then, is the great revelation: the church and the synagogue were never to be separated; they were always meant to be together. In God's eyes, new believers who were once Gentiles were now adopted members of His house and were expected to be in community alongside their Jewish brothers and sisters to worship and hear the Word. Look again at Ephesians 2:

> *For He Himself is our peace, who has made both one, and has broken down the middle wall of separation, having abolished in His flesh the enmity, that is, the law of commandments contained in ordinances, so as to create in Himself one new man from the two, thus making peace, and that He might reconcile them both to God in one body through the cross, thereby putting to death the enmity.* (Ephesians 2:14–16)

Jesus is *"our peace"* who has made both Jew and Gentile one. He has broken down the middle wall that divided us. Remembering that everything God does has a physical side and a spiritual side, I believe that one day soon God will rebuild His physical temple in Jerusalem. For the time being, however, He is at work building His spiritual temple within the hearts of His people.

This is not unlike the tabernacle of David's day, which was a temporary forerunner of the permanent temple that Solomon would build. This portable tabernacle was remarkable for two reasons.

First, it instituted a new order of worship. King David recognized that Israel had a tendency to see animal sacrifices as a substitute for piety.

Many, O Lord my God, are Your wonderful works which You have done....Sacrifice and offering You did not desire; my ears You have opened. Burnt offering and sin offering You did not require. Then I said, "Behold, I come; in the scroll of the book it is written of me. I delight to do Your will, O my God, and Your law is within my heart."
(Psalm 40:5–8)

Not content to only offer animal sacrifices, David also urged people to bring their entire selves—bodies, spirits, and souls—to the altar with praise offerings of singing, hand clapping, shouting, dancing, and instruments.

Clap your hands, all you peoples! Shout to God with the voice of triumph!...Sing praises to God, sing praises! Sing praises to our King, sing praises! For God is the King of all the earth; sing praises with understanding.   (Psalm 47:1, 6–7)

O Lord, open my lips, and my mouth shall show forth Your praise. For You do not desire sacrifice, or else I would give it; You do not delight in burnt offering. The sacrifices of God are a broken spirit, a broken and a contrite heart; these, O God, You will not despise. (Psalm 51:15–17)

In our spiritual tabernacle, therefore, there is no longer a need for offering sacrifices, because Jesus has been sacrificed for us.

He was oppressed and He was afflicted, yet He opened not His mouth; He was led as a lamb to the slaughter, and as a sheep before its shearers is silent, so He opened not His mouth.   (Isaiah 53:7)

Instead, like David, we offer our entire selves to God in service and worship. We realize that God is more interested in our hearts than in empty activities and rituals.

Second, within the physical tabernacle, there was a barrier between God and man. Only the high priest could enter through the curtain of the Holy of Holies to go before God, and only on one day a year—the Day of Atonement. At the very moment when Jesus died, however, that very curtain was ripped in half from top to bottom.

> *Then, behold, the veil of the temple was torn in two from top to bottom; and the earth quaked, and the rocks were split.* (Matthew 27:51)

In the epistles, the author of Hebrews taught the early church that they no longer needed a high priest as an intermediary to offer sacrifices before God for the people.

> *Seeing then that we have a great High Priest who has passed through the heavens, Jesus the Son of God, let us hold fast our confession. For we do not have a High Priest who cannot sympathize with our weaknesses, but was in all points tempted as we are, yet without sin. Let us therefore come boldly to the throne of grace, that we may obtain mercy and find grace to help in time of need.* (Hebrews 4:14–16)

They already had a high priest, Jesus, who had offered the ultimate sacrifice—His own life. Now, through Him, you and I have direct access to the power and throne of God!

Now, we can clearly see that our *spiritual tabernacle* is two-thirds built. The sacrifice has been paid. The barrier has been torn down, and we can come boldly into the presence of God's power. There is only one thing left. Look again at Ephesians 2:14: *"He Himself is our peace, who has made both one, and has broken down the middle wall of separation."*

We need to recognize that Jesus tore down the wall between Jew and Gentile. Unfortunately, it seems that we have been trying hard to rebuild it ever since. What a tragedy! How this must pain the heart of God, especially when His goal seems to be reunification:

> *Till we all come to the unity of the faith and of the knowledge of the Son of God, to a perfect man, to the measure of the stature of the fullness of Christ.* (Ephesians 4:13)

Perhaps it will be in our lifetimes that God will call His people to tear down the wall of division that separates Israel and the Gentile church. This is where it gets exciting! You may be thinking, *How will this happen, and how can I be a part of this great end-time prophecy?*

When we add to our faith knowledge (an understanding of the Jewish Torah), and the Jews add to their knowledge faith (a belief in Jesus as the Messiah), then we will become that one new man—perfect and complete. Together, we will see the fullness of Christ come about in our lives, and the temple of God will be complete.

This is the key to the great, final outpouring of God's power. Let it start with us. Let us, as Christians, be the ones who get the anointing flowing. Let us begin tearing down what separates us by adding to *our* faith *their* knowledge. Let's reveal the mystery so we can receive the miracles. Let's uncover *The Torah Blessing.*

3

Grace and the Law:
The Arrow That Points to Jesus

s we discovered in the last chapter, in order to be built together for a dwelling place of God—the temple of God—our foundation must be composed of both the prophets (the Old Testament) and the apostles (the New Testament). It's very important that we understand this concept. For us to understand the teachings of Jesus, Paul, Peter, James, or any of the apostles of the New Testament, we first have to understand Abraham, Moses, David, Isaiah, and the rest of the prophets of the Old Testament.

You might say that the stronger our Christian faith becomes, the more Jewish we should regard ourselves. Dr. Richard Booker wrote:

> The Bible is a Hebrew book, telling the story of the Hebrew people. Jesus was a Hebrew Lord. We, on the other hand, are Western people sharing a very diverse and sometimes controversial heritage that comes from many sources. If the Bible is going to be understood in our day, we must develop "Hebrew eyes" and "Hebrew attitudes" toward life.[1]

Author and rabbi Stuart E. Rosenberg agrees, "The stronger a man's Christian faith, the more Jewish will he regard himself."[2] Swiss theologian Karl Barth wrote, "The Bible...is a Jewish book. It cannot be read

---

[1] Dr. Richard Booker, "Why Should Christians Learn about Jews and Jewish Traditions?" from the Institute for Hebraic-Christian Studies, 1998, http://www.haydid.org/update714a.htm.
[2] Stuart E. Rosenberg, *The Christian Problem: A Jewish View* (New York: Hippocrene Books, 1986), 222–223.

and understood and expounded unless we are prepared to become Jews with the Jews."[3] In 1938, Pope Pius XI delivered an encyclical against racism in which he wrote, "Spiritually we are all Semites."

> ## Our Bible is *not* composed of two different covenants or testaments, but one.

This is in line with what God said to me in Israel over a decade ago: "Larry, I will open your eyes, and you will begin to read My words, not through the eyes of a *Gentile* Jesus, but through the eyes of a *Jewish* Jesus."

Believe it or not, our Bible is *not* composed of two different covenants or testaments, but one. Look at what Jesus taught us in Matthew 26:28:

For this is My blood of the new covenant, which is shed for many for the remission of sins.

Here, the word *new* doesn't mean "different"; it means "fresh." You may wonder at this point, *Doesn't the Bible say we have a* better *covenant?* (See Hebrews 7:22; 8:6.) Yes, it's better, but it's not different. The first covenant was given to Moses and written on stone.

The LORD said to Moses, "Come up to Me on the mountain and be there; and I will give you tablets of stone, and the law and commandments which I have written, that you may teach them." (Exodus 24:12)

And when He had made an end of speaking with him on Mount Sinai, He gave Moses two tablets of the Testimony, tablets of stone, written with the finger of God. (Exodus 31:18)

The New Testament was a new covenant—a fresh covenant—written on our hearts because of Jesus Christ. Not different; definitely better.

This is the covenant that I will make with them after those days, says the LORD: I will put My laws into their hearts, and in their minds I will write them. (Hebrews 10:16)

---

[3] Karl Barth, *Church Dogmatics*, trans. by Geoffrey W. Bromiley et al. (Edinburgh: T. & T. Clark, 1956), 511.

The Law: Curse or Blessing?

One of the most debated and confusing concepts in Christianity centers around the issues of God's grace and His precepts—what we might call "the law." At first glance, even Scripture seems to have a hard time wrestling with this issue. For instance, in this passage, the apostle Paul made the law seem pretty grim:

> *Now we know that whatever the law says, it says to those who are under the law, that every mouth may be stopped, and all the world may become guilty before God. Therefore by the deeds of the law no flesh will be justified in His sight, for by the law is the knowledge of sin. But now the righteousness of God apart from the law is revealed...through faith in Jesus Christ, to all and on all who believe.*   (Romans 3:19–22)

According to Paul, our righteousness is apart from the law. Then, only a few verses later, he declared:

> *Do we then make void the law through faith? Certainly not! On the contrary, we establish the law.*   (verse 31)

Thus, we are righteous apart from the law, but we are also to *"establish the law."* Paul was asking the question: "Is the law now obsolete because we are saved by grace?" Rhetorically, he answered his own question: *"Certainly not! On the contrary...."*

Later in Romans, Paul discussed how we are to deal with temptation and whether or not we answer to the law:

> *Therefore do not let sin reign in your mortal body, that you should obey it in its lusts. And do not present your members as instruments of unrighteousness to sin, but present yourselves to God as being alive from the dead, and your members as instruments of righteousness to God. For sin shall not have dominion over you, for you are not under law but under grace. What then? Shall we sin because we are not under law but under grace? Certainly not!*   (Romans 6:12–15)

Once again, Paul asked and answered his own question. First, he urged readers not to let sin rule over their bodies but instead to present themselves as instruments of righteousness. He went on to say that sin has no power over us as Christians, for we are *"not under law but under grace."* Then, Paul addressed "the elephant in the room" by asking the crucial question: "Is sin permissible since we are *'not under law but under grace'*?" After all, if we are saved by grace and not by works, doesn't that grace give us the liberty to live without boundaries—without obligation to God and His law? *"Certainly not!"* Paul concluded.

Under the Curse

This may seem like going around in circles to you. If anything has been made clear, it is that we are under grace, but we still must deal with God's law. Let us, therefore, begin to get a handle on a healthy relationship between grace and the law.

> *God sent forth His Son, born of a woman, born under the law, to redeem those who were under the law, that we might receive the adoption as sons.* (Galatians 4:4–5)

Paul said Jesus was to redeem those who were—there it is again—*"under the law."* Why? He redeemed them so they might be adopted, grafted in, as sons of God.

> *For as many as are of the works of the law are **under the curse**; for it is written, "Cursed is everyone who does not continue in all things which are written in the book of the law, to do them." But that no one is justified by the law in the sight of God is evident, for "the just shall live by faith."…Christ has redeemed us from the curse of the law, having become a curse for us.* (Galatians 3:10–11, 13, emphasis added)

Here again, Paul implied that the law is a curse. Then, in Romans, he seemed to do a complete about-face:

> *Therefore the law is holy, and the commandment holy and just and good.* (Romans 7:12)

On one hand, we are saved by grace, and we are not under the curse of the law; on the other hand, the law is *"holy and just and good."* Was Paul schizophrenic? Not at all. Let me explain.

The apostle Paul was the only writer in the entire Bible who used the term *"under the law."* He was also the only one to refer to the law as a curse. These statements are *idioms*. An idiom doesn't usually mean exactly what it says on the surface. A couple of modern examples would be, "He has a chip on his shoulder," or, "That guy kicked the bucket." These are expressions. There is, in reality, no actual *chip* or *bucket*.

Torah versus Nomos

Obviously, not everyone who obeyed the commandments of God was *"under the curse of the law."* Jesus obeyed God's laws, as did Paul himself. Certainly, they were not cursed. In Hebrew, the word for *law* is *torah*, meaning "to teach," denoting a map or pathway to learning. In this context, *"the law"* was not so much about rules and behavior but more about a mentoring relationship as children of God. In Greek, the word for *law* is *nomos*. In the Greek context, the law is more about legalism—the *dos* and *don'ts* to achieve favor or disfavor.

> **Beyond a shadow of a doubt, it's by faith that we are saved—not by works.**

Are we saved by grace? The answer is yes, absolutely! Beyond a shadow of a doubt, it's by faith that we are saved—and not by works.

> *For by grace you have been saved through faith, and that not of your-selves; it is the gift of God, not of works, lest anyone should boast.*
> (Ephesians 2:8–9)

There is no list of behaviors—*nomos*—by which we can overcome our own sins and make ourselves acceptable before a holy God. We are saved only by faith in Jesus Christ as Lord and Savior. That said, it doesn't mean we can't be taught by God's law—*torah*. Now that I'm forgiven, born again, washed in His blood, grafted into His family, and made an heir to His covenant, is it okay for me to steal? Can I begin to worship idols? Paul's answer was, in effect, "God forbid!"

Why, then, did he refer to the law as *"the curse"*? The answer: it's not God's teachings that are cursed; it's what man does with them. Let me give you an example. Should a Christian tithe? Of course he should. Why? Because to withhold it is to steal from God and shut the window of God's blessings from heaven.

"Will a man rob God? Yet you have robbed Me! But you say, 'In what way have we robbed You?' In tithes and offerings. You are cursed with a curse, for you have robbed Me, even this whole nation. Bring all the tithes into the storehouse, that there may be food in My house, and try Me now in this," says the LORD of hosts, "if I will not open for you the windows of heaven and pour out for you such blessing that there will not be room enough to receive it." (Malachi 3:8–10)

Does tithing save you? No. God, therefore, gave us a law—a *torah*, or teaching—not to give us a way to earn our salvation, but to give us a pathway to connect our lives with God's prosperity. When a man, Jew or Gentile, takes God's teachings—*torah*—and turns them into legalism—*nomos*—they then become a curse.

When I was first saved by asking Jesus into my heart, I was taught that on the one hand, I was saved by grace, but on the other hand, it was made very clear that if I didn't tithe, I wasn't *really* saved. I later learned that this was wrong; I had been misled. God's teaching on tithing, meant for my own benefit and blessing, had been turned into the bondage of religious legalism. In Matthew 23, Jesus rebuked this kind of thinking:

Woe to you, scribes and Pharisees, hypocrites! For you are like white-washed tombs which indeed appear beautiful outwardly, but inside are full of dead men's bones and all uncleanness. Even so you also outwardly appear righteous to men, but inside you are full of hypocrisy and lawlessness. (Matthew 23:27–28)

Jesus essentially told them, "You are doing all the right things on the outside, but on the inside you're full of '*hypocrisy and lawlessness.*'" They were keeping God's laws to the best of their ability, yet in God's eyes they were still considered lawless. How could this be?

Religion versus Revelation

What does the Torah teach us? How is it guiding us along the pathway? Jesus told us in the previous chapter,

> *"Teacher, which is the great commandment in the law?" Jesus said to him, "'You shall love the LORD your God with all your heart, with all your soul, and with all your mind.' This is the first and great commandment. And the second is like it: 'You shall love your neighbor as yourself.' On these two commandments hang all the Law and the Prophets."* (Matthew 22:36–40)

In this passage, a Pharisee had come to see if Jesus was teaching something new and different from the Torah. To test Jesus, he asked, "What is the greatest commandment in all the law?" Jesus responded by telling the man to love God with all his heart, soul, and mind. But Jesus didn't stop there. He went on to say that there was another commandment of equal importance: to love your neighbor as you love yourself. Jesus finished by saying that these two commandments encapsulate everything in the Torah and the prophets had taught. Every law, every parable, and every prophecy leads to two things: love God and love your neighbor.

Why, then, did Jesus later rebuke the Pharisees as *"whitewashed tombs"*? He did so because following the letter of the law hadn't taught these men anything about loving God or loving their neighbors. It was merely religious exercise, and in their strict legalism, their pride had led them to use the law to reject, condemn, and even hate others. This was not God's purpose for His people. This was simply the religion of man.

Living the Torah

A few years ago, my wife, Tiz, and I took a group on one of our many trips to Israel. We all had a day off of touring in order to do some shopping in Jerusalem. A few days later, I was told that an orthodox Jewish man had spit at Tiz on that day. By the time I was told, we had traveled all the way to the Sea of Galilee in Tiberias. Our traveling party knew that if I had known this in Jerusalem, I might have lost my temper and shown that man a whole new meaning of the term "the laying on of hands." Because of Tiz's short, blonde hair and modern, Western appearance, this man had spit at her. As a devout, orthodox Jew, he dressed only in black, wore a *tallit*—or prayer shawl—and didn't shave the sides of his beard. I'm sure he faithfully observed the Sabbath, as well as many other Jewish traditions. In his actions toward Tiz, however, this man showed no love for God. His behavior was exactly the kind of thing Jesus was talking about. The purpose of the Torah is not to make us into religious, legalistic, and intolerant robots on the outside. When that happens, Paul said we come *"under the curse of the law."*

By comparison, we later met two wonderful Jewish men of God in Venice, Italy. These two men were almost identical in appearance to the man Tiz encountered in Jerusalem. Thankfully, their hearts were much different. We were in Venice's historic Jewish ghetto—the place where the word *ghetto* originated. I was waiting for Tiz outside a shop when these two young men approached and started talking to me. They asked about my prayer life and wanted to know if I had prayed that day. When I told them I had, they asked, "Have you prayed with *tefillin?*" This is the Hebrew practice of wrapping a strap of leather around your arm and another around your head when you pray. These men showed me Deuteronomy 6, where God instructed His people to pray this way.

I told them, "If you can tell me why you do this, not just out of ritual or legalism but from the true meaning of it, then I'll pray it with you." They smiled and said, "First, it slows us down and reminds us to think, *I'm about to talk to almighty God. He has invited me to talk with Him. He will stop all that He is doing, not only to listen to me, but also to speak back to me in my heart. Instead of being so busy, therefore, I need to slow down. God, my Father in heaven, wants to spend time with me.* Next, it reminds us that there are others who don't know God, who don't know that He loves them and wants to talk to them, too. I can't be satisfied that I, alone, talk to Him; I must also tell others."

> I can't be satisfied that I, alone, talk to God; I must also tell others.

Needless to say, we prayed together that day in Venice. I told them that I was a Christian pastor. It didn't matter to them. We had a wonderful, loving discussion based on mutual respect and increased understanding. As we took the time to love and pray for each other, we were also loving God. It was such a stark contrast to the angry assault Tiz experienced in Jerusalem. That day, the wall between Jew and Gentile was reduced a little more.

The prayer these two men referred to is called the *Shema* in Hebrew, and it is found in Deuteronomy 6:

Hear, O Israel: The LORD our God, the LORD is one! You shall love the LORD your God with all your heart, with all your soul, and with all your strength. And these words which I command you today shall be in your heart. You shall teach them diligently to your children, and shall talk of them when you sit in your house, when you walk by the way, when you lie down, and when you rise up. You shall bind them as a sign on your hand, and they shall be as frontlets between your eyes. You shall write them on the doorposts of your house and on your gates.

(verses 4–9)

Twice a day, an observant Jew is to pray, "Hear, O Israel: the Lord is our God, the Lord is One. You shall love Him with all your heart, with all your soul, and with all your strength." This is very important to the Jewish people and is actually the source of most misunderstandings between Jews and Christians.

Recently, I was on an airplane with Matt and Laurie Crouch of TBN. They had interviewed rabbis on television and engaged them in matters of faith. They said, "These rabbis are fellowshipping with us, but they are not really listening to us. How do we get these rabbis to listen to us?"

I offered them one piece of advice: don't pray to Jesus. This may sound absurd at first, but let's remember what Jesus said:

And in that day you will ask Me nothing. Most assuredly, I say to you, whatever you ask the Father in My name He will give you.

(John 16:23)

In other words, Jesus was saying, "Don't pray to Me. I will pay the price so that you may boldly go before the Father." Jesus even taught us exactly how to pray:

So He said to them, "When you pray, say: Our Father in heaven…."

(Luke 11:2)

This is so important when dealing with Jews, whose entire faith is based upon the Shema prayer: "Hear, O Israel: the Lord is our God, the Lord is One." Jesus is our Messiah and the Son of God. He is our Savior, the Passover Lamb who paid the price so that the Holy of Holies would be opened up and we might go directly before the throne of God.

The Shema is what Jesus was referring to in Matthew 22.

One of them, a lawyer, asked Him a question, testing Him, and saying, "Teacher, which is the great commandment in the law?" Jesus said to him, "'You shall love the Lord your God with all your heart, with all your soul, and with all your mind.' This is the first and great commandment." (verses 35–38)

Remember, however, that Jesus added a second commandment of equal importance. *"And the second is like it: 'You shall love your neighbor as yourself.' On these two commandments hang all the Law and the Prophets"* (verses 39–40). Love God, yes, but love your neighbor, too.

Now by this we know that we know Him, if we keep His commandments. He who says, "I know Him," and does not keep His commandments, is a liar, and the truth is not in him. (1 John 2:3–4)

What are *"His commandments"*? According to Jesus, it all boils down to loving God and loving your neighbor as yourself.

No one has seen God at any time. If we love one another, God abides in us, and His love has been perfected in us. (1 John 4:12)

If we love one another, it shows the world that we are not just religious but that the love of God lives within us. His love, His teachings, His Torah, His path, and His law have been *"perfected in us."*

If someone says, "I love God," and hates his brother, he is a liar; for he who does not love his brother whom he has seen, how can he love God whom he has not seen? And this commandment we have from Him: that he who loves God must love his brother also. (1 John 4:20–21)

Now tell me, of these two experiences—the man in Jerusalem and the two men in Venice—who had religion, and who had God's revelation? Who was *"under the curse of the law,"* and who was living out the Torah love of God and love of neighbor—even when that neighbor was a Christian pastor from the other side of the world? Who had legalism? Who had liberty?

Jesus came to teach us to walk on God's path.

Do not think that I came to destroy the Law or the Prophets. I did not come to destroy but to fulfill. (Matthew 5:17)

Torah, as we learned, means "teacher, guide, path," but it also refers to the first five books in the Bible: Genesis, Exodus, Leviticus, Numbers, and Deuteronomy. Jesus said, in effect, "I didn't come to destroy the five books of Moses or the prophets and all they taught but to teach, fulfill, and empower you, through the Holy Spirit, to walk in the Torah."

Let your light so shine before men, that they may see your good works and glorify your Father in heaven. (verse 16)

How does our light shine? Does it shine by being religious and legalistic? Or does it shine by living out the Torah through loving God and loving one another? The only way to bring light into the darkness is to let the world see your life and, in turn, glorify your Father in heaven. Jesus didn't come to stop us from fulfilling the Torah but to put us back on the Torah path, where we become rays of light in a darkened world.

> **The only way to bring light into darkness is to let the world see your life and, in turn, glorify your Father in heaven.**

The Ten Mitzvahs

In Hebrew, the word for *commandment* is *mitzvah*. In Judaism, there are 613 mitzvahs. All of these mitzvahs are encompassed by the Ten Commandments. Today, there seems to be a concerted attempt to remove all public representations of the Ten Commandments from schools, courthouses, and even our nation's capitol.

Let's take a brief refresher course on the Ten Commandments that God gave Moses on Mount Sinai, as recorded in Exodus 20:

1. You shall have no other gods before Him.

2. You shall not make for yourself a carved image or any likeness—an idol.

3. You shall not to take the name of the Lord in vain.

4. You shall remember the Sabbath day and keep it holy.

5. You shall honor your father and your mother.

6. You shall not murder.

7. You shall not commit adultery.

8. You shall not steal.

9. You shall not bear false witness against your neighbor.

10. You shall not covet your neighbor's house or anything that is your neighbor's.

These Ten Commandments are encompassed in the two commandments (mitzvahs) Jesus gave us in Matthew 22:

"You shall love the LORD your God with all your heart, with all your soul, and with all your mind." This is the first and great commandment. And the second is like it: "You shall love your neighbor as yourself." On these two commandments hang all the Law and the Prophets.
(Matthew 22:37–40)

When you look at the Ten Commandments as a list, it is easy to see where they are divided into the same two categories Jesus referred to. The first four commandments deal with man loving God. The last six deal with man loving his neighbor.

Have you accepted Jesus Christ as your Lord and Savior?

Yes? Good.

Does this mean that since you are saved by grace, you don't have to follow these Ten Commandments? Does it mean that Jesus put an end to those teachings? Or does it mean what Jesus said, in effect, in Matthew 5:

"I haven't come to destroy these paths of blessing, but to show you how to walk in this path"?

Fortunately for us, all 613 mitzvahs have been condensed into these two mitzvahs: love God, and love others as yourself. How simple! How wonderful!

I wish I were a perfect man, a perfect Christian, a perfect husband, and a perfect father, but I'm not. Even though I'm saved by grace and not by anything I've done or will ever do, I still need God's mercy and His Word to keep me from getting lost. Should we do away with God's Torah? God forbid. His Word keeps us on the path!

The Law Points the Way

Let's go back to the seesaw arguments of Paul as he dealt with faith and works, grace and the law.

> *Christ is the end of the law for righteousness to everyone who believes. For Moses writes about the righteousness which is of the law, "The man who does those things shall live by them."* (Romans 10:4–5)

Paul made it clear that Jesus is *"the end of the law."* Here, *end* does not mean "finished." It can't. After all, as I just stated, the law is not over. What Paul was saying is that all of God's laws—the Torah—have *pointed* out our need for Jesus, our Savior and Messiah, and our need for God's amazing, saving grace. I like to say that we should think of the word *end* in this verse not as a finish line but as the end, or tip, of an arrow. In this case, the Torah becomes the arrow that points us to Jesus. That's why Jesus said, *"If you believed Moses, you would believe Me; for he wrote about Me"* (John 5:46).

Mitzvahs and Tzedakahs

In Romans, Paul said that Moses wrote about the righteousness of the law—the Torah, the teaching, the path. In this case, *righteousness* does not refer to correct behavior. It doesn't mean, "I don't smoke, cuss, chew, or go out with those who do." It doesn't mean following a rigid, legalistic set of rules. In Hebrew, the word *righteousness* is *tzedakah*, meaning "charity, justice, or fairness." The Ten Commandments accurately reflect both the spiritual and earthly sides of God: to love Him and to love our fellow men. Righteousness also has two sides: *mitzvahs*—loving and serving God, and *tzedakah*—acts of kindness, love, and charity toward our neighbors.

Moses wrote that the man who does these things shall live by them. (See Leviticus 18:5.) As a Christian, I had always heard, "If you're going to keep any of the laws, you have to keep all of the law." That's not what Paul said. If you look to the law—*nomos*—for your salvation, then, yes, you must keep all of the law. That is what is called "living under the law," which is a curse. But the Torah that is "the path" will lead us into Jesus' redemptive shedding of blood. The man who does acts of charity and kindness for his neighbors shall find life. Every teaching and law God gives us is not only to love Him but also to follow His mitzvah by loving our neighbors with tzedakah.

> **The man who does acts of charity and kindness for his neighbors shall find life.**

On the Mount

When Moses received God's ten mitzvahs, he had to go up on the mountain. Likewise, when Jesus preached his greatest sermon, he did so on a mountain. His Sermon on the Mount includes some of the most well-known portions of Scripture. When seen through Jewish eyes, however, His words seem to change from a Sunday school lesson into something much more powerful.

> *You are the salt of the earth; but if the salt loses its flavor, how shall it be seasoned? It is then good for nothing but to be thrown out and trampled underfoot by men. You are the light of the world. A city that is set on a hill cannot be hidden. Nor do they light a lamp and put it under a basket, but on a lampstand, and it gives light to all who are in the house. Let your light so shine before men, that they may see your good works and glorify your Father in heaven.*

> *Do not think that I came to destroy the Law or the Prophets. I did not come to destroy but to fulfill. For assuredly, I say to you, till heaven and*

earth pass away, one jot or one tittle will by no means pass from the law till all is fulfilled. Whoever therefore breaks one of the least of these commandments, and teaches men so, shall be called least in the kingdom of heaven; but whoever does and teaches them, he shall be called great in the kingdom of heaven. For I say to you, that unless your righteousness exceeds the righteousness of the scribes and Pharisees, you will by no means enter the kingdom of heaven.   (Matthew 5:13–20)

Jesus explained that His Jewish followers were meant to be lights in a dark world, where they were to shine as examples. According to Jesus, when the world saw their good works—their mitzvahs—it would bless all other nations and connect them with the kingdom of God. Jesus made it clear that He did not come to destroy this but to put His followers back on this path. Their acts of charity—their tzedakahs—would serve to teach others to be lights, as well, and they would all be called great in the kingdom of heaven. The righteousness of the Jews—their mitzvahs and tzedakahs— should exceed the phony righteousness demonstrated by the piously religious who knew only how to condemn, judge, and divide. To the world, the difference was obvious.

Jesus continued His teaching:

Therefore I say to you, do not worry about your life, what you will eat or what you will drink; nor about your body, what you will put on. Is not life more than food and the body more than clothing? Look at the birds of the air, for they neither sow nor reap nor gather into barns; yet your heavenly Father feeds them. Are you not of more value than they? Which of you by worrying can add one cubit to his stature? So why do you worry about clothing? Consider the lilies of the field, how they grow: they neither toil nor spin; and yet I say to you that even Solomon in all his glory was not arrayed like one of these. Now if God so clothes the grass of the field, which today is, and tomorrow is thrown into the oven, will He not much more clothe you, O you of little faith? Therefore do not worry, saying, "What shall we eat?" or "What shall we drink?" or "What shall we wear?" For after all these things the Gentiles seek. For your heavenly Father knows that you need all these things.
(Matthew 6:25–32)

Jesus said, in effect, "Don't worry about your life, what you have to eat, or how you will clothe and shelter your family. That is what the Gentiles worry about." Now that we are grafted in as part of God's family—children of abundance and heirs to the promise—we no longer have to worry about those things, either.

> But seek first the kingdom of God and His righteousness, and all these things shall be added to you. (Matthew 6:33)

Seek First...

Owen lives in Oregon and is one of my best friends. He and a group of friends meet together each Sunday and Wednesday to have church with New Beginnings through our streaming broadcast on the Internet. They worship and pray along with us. They send in tithes and offerings. They follow along with the teaching on Jewish roots. They are a part of our congregation as much as anyone else who walks through our doors in Dallas.

For quite some time, Owen had been trying to sell his house. Unfortunately, the real estate market in Oregon has been hit hard by the downturn in the economy, just as many other areas have been. Recently, while watching one of our services on his computer, Owen felt the Lord urging him to donate an extra offering to the ministry as a faith seed for the selling of his house. Owen obeyed the leading and sent the offering that day.

The next week, Owen was praying intently and felt led by the Lord to visit his bank in an attempt to refinance his mortgage until the home sold. At the bank, Owen began to tell the banker all about his house. Suddenly, the banker became very excited. He said, "That is exactly the kind of house I've been looking for. Can I buy it from you?" Within two weeks, Owen closed the sale on his home. He then flew to Dallas to bring a tithe and firstfruit offering from the sale. He was obedient when he felt God's leading, and God was faithful to provide for his needs.

As children of God, we have to concern ourselves only with two things. First, on the heavenly side, we prioritize God's mitzvahs in our lives. The Shema says, "Hear, O Israel (that includes us): the Lord is our God, the Lord is One. You shall love Him with all your heart, with all your soul, and with all your strength." Second, on the earthly side, we are to seek His righteousness—tzedakah—His acts of kindness, charity, and love toward our neighbors.

Then what? Then, *"all these things shall be added to you."* What are these things? They include the things we once spent our lives worrying about: food, clothing, shelter, possessions, and finances. Jesus acknowledged our need for these things and acknowledged that the Gentiles focused on them, yet He emphasized that God's children are not to spend time and effort trying to obtain them. We are to live with constant vigilance for any opportunity to be God's lights in a dark world. If we prioritize God and His righteousness, God is faithful to care for our needs.

> **If we prioritize God and His righteousness, He is faithful to care for our needs.**

The steps of a good man are ordered by the LORD, *and He delights in his way. Though he fall, he shall not be utterly cast down; for the* LORD *upholds him with His hand. I have been young, and now am old; yet I have not seen the righteous forsaken, nor His descendants begging bread. He is ever merciful, and lends; and His descendants are blessed.* (Psalm 37:23–26)

That Scripture says it all. First, the steps of a good man are *"ordered"*— put on a path—to lead and teach him. The righteous—those who do acts of tzedakah, or charity—will not be forsaken. Those who show mercy to others will see their seeds—their children and grandchildren—blessed.

All These Things Shall Be Added to You

Christine is a member of New Beginnings who has been learning and applying the teaching of Jewish roots to her life for several years. The teachings of the mitzvah and tzedakah have truly taken root in her heart. She learned firsthand that as we honor God by doing acts of charity and kindness to others, God promises to honor and care for us.

Several months ago, Christine met an elderly woman named Claire who was disabled and bedridden. Christine immediately felt the leading that God had brought Claire into her life so that she could demonstrate the love of God. Christine began to pour her time and energies into Claire's life, and a tremendous love and friendship began to build between the two women. Her acts of kindness (tzedakah) served to enrich both of their lives.

But that's not the end of the story. Recently, Claire passed away and went to be with the Lord. Christine mourned her friend's passing and missed her deeply. She felt honored to have been given the opportunity to be a blessing in Claire's life during her last days on earth. A few days later, Christine opened her mailbox to discover an unexpected surprise. Claire had left Christine ten thousand dollars from her estate. What a wonderful reminder that when we put the needs of others before our own, God promises that He will see to it that all of our needs are met.

More than merely an outer ritual, the Torah teaches us to live as God's children on the inside—in our hearts. In living out the Torah, we shine a light into the darkness of the world and point others toward the goodness, mercy, and love of Christ.

As we go forward, I'd like to focus not so much on God's *don't*s as His *do*s. There is a misperception out there that a life with God is dominated by all the things you are forbidden from doing. What a lie! A life with God is completely saturated by all the activities, adventures, and blessings that you *get* to experience. Unfortunately, many of the very activities and practices that God gave to His people as ways to better connect with Him have been forsaken and abandoned throughout the centuries. As you will see, these are not obscure rabbinical teachings hidden in Jewish lore and oral tradition but God's direct teachings and commands in our Old Testament, which Christians have written off, along with the Jews themselves.

4

The Missing Piece to a 2000-Year-Old Puzzle: Tearing Down the Wall

The people…will hear all these statutes [the Torah], and say, "Surely this great nation [Israel] is a wise and understanding people. For what great nation is there that has a God so near to it, as is the LORD our God is to us, for whatever reason we may call upon Him?"

(Deuteronomy 4:6–7)

Recently Tiz and I were having dinner with some good friends and fellow ministers. They couldn't wait to tell us about what had just happened to them. A man they had met—a fellow minister—had come over to their house for dinner on a Friday evening. As they sat down to eat, the man asked, "Could I show you something that will bring a great blessing on you, your home, and your family?" He then went on to teach them about *Shabbat*, the blessing of the Sabbath.

Later, as they told me about that evening, my friends said, "Larry, it was absolutely amazing, the joy, the peace, and the presence of the Lord that we felt that night. It was like we found a missing piece of the puzzle."

They were understandably excited. You see, the Sabbath is not about following some old rules from long ago; it is a day in every week—an appointed time—that the Lord has set aside to bless us and everything we put our hands to with His supernatural power.

My friends' excitement, however, became tempered by concern. "Larry, how do we explain this to others—our family and friends?" Both sides of their families had a long line of relatives involved in ministry who, like most of us, were familiar with both Galatians 3:10, which talks about being under the curse of the law, and Galatians 3:13, which states that *"Christ has redeemed us from the curse of the law."* Our friends then said, "If we try to tell our families what we experienced on that Sabbath, we know that they will say that it was only Old Testament legalism—that we are not under *"the curse of the law"* any more.

You have probably heard similar arguments. How, then, do we explain it? What are we to say? Since Jesus paid the price for our sins and we are saved by grace and not by works (see Ephesians 2:8–9), are we no longer required to follow the laws of God? None? Not any of them? Are we *"under the curse"* (Galatians 3:10) when we *"have no other gods"* (Exodus 20:3) before Him? Or what about *"You shall not commit adultery"* (verse 14) or *"You shall not steal"* (verse 15)? By following these "laws" of God are we *cursed* or are we *blessed*? Are we saved by grace and not by works? Are we better off or worse off? I think we would all agree that not only are our marriages, families, and lives much better off when we live according to God's Word—His Torah, His path, and His law—but our society and the world as a whole are a much better place.

So what do we say to people? Perhaps God is moving us from the milk (the elementary teachings of God's Word such as no other gods, no stealing, no murder, no adultery) to the meat (the deeper things of God, like Exodus 20:8: *"Remember the Sabbath and keep it holy."*) (See 1 Corinthians 3:2 KJV.) Is God's Torah a curse that we don't have to understand anymore, or is God's Torah a path we can walk upon and not get lost in this world in which we live? In this chapter, I'll show you the answer to these questions. It's so simple that you will wonder why you haven't seen it before. It truly is *the missing piece to a 2,000-year-old puzzle.*

Three Supernatural Elements to the Tabernacle of David

We have already discussed the tabernacle of David, but let us briefly look at what the Lord says about this spiritual miracle and the second coming of Jesus, of the Messiah. Look with me again at the prophecy of Jews and Gentiles worshipping the God of Abraham, Isaac, and Jacob together.

"On that day I will raise up the tabernacle of David, which has fallen down, and repair its damages; I will raise up its ruins, and rebuild it as in the days of old; that they may possess the remnant of Edom, and all the Gentiles who are called by My name," says the LORD *who does this thing.* (Amos 9:11–12)

Now let's go to Ephesians 2:13–14:

But now in Christ Jesus you who once were far off have been brought near by the blood of Christ. For He Himself is our peace, who has made both one, and has broken down the middle wall of separation.

Without going into greater detail about the tabernacle of David and what it all means, let's look at the three main "power points" that made the tabernacle of David so special. Why? Because what God did then, He is ready to do now in an even greater outpouring of His anointing.

"The glory of this latter temple shall be greater than the former," says the LORD *of hosts. "And in this place I will give peace," says the* LORD *of hosts.* (Haggai 2:9)

The first thing we see in the first tabernacle of David was the *continual* presence of God's supernatural power. Second, there was supernaturally anointed music and worship. Without spending a lot of time again on this, God is ready to do it again. We are ready right now for the *latter rain.* The worship in your church can become so anointed by God that He will begin to do miracles as people walk in the doors. As I'm sitting at my desk writing this, I can feel God's prophetic anointing on me. Not only will God's power be so great that people will feel His power as they walk in the doors, but even as people are driving by, God will draw them to your churches for salvation and miracles.

So, let's review again what will happen as you and I rebuild the tabernacle of David: 1) there will be supernaturally anointed worship, which will lead to, 2) signs, wonders, and miracles, the power of God "24/7" in your life, which will lead to, 3) no middle wall—Jews and Gentiles will be worshipping together.

For He Himself is our peace, who has made both one, and has broken down the middle wall of separation.   (Ephesians 2:14)

No middle wall, nothing is dividing us—Jew and Gentile.

Having abolished in His flesh the enmity, that is, the law of command-ments contained in ordinances, so as to create in Himself one new man from the two, thus making peace.   (verse 15)

"One new man from the two." The two—Jew and Gentile—become "*one new man*", a new house of God.

Having been built on the foundation of the apostles and prophets, Jesus Christ Himself being the chief corner stone, in whom the whole build-ing, being joined together, grows into a holy temple in the Lord.
(verses 21–21)

We are building the house of God—the tabernacle of David—upon the teaching of the apostles (New Testament) and the prophets (Old Testament or the Torah) with Jesus serving as *"the chief cornerstone"*, the *piece* that connects the two—*joining us together.*

The Problem and the Answer

When we look at the challenge of bringing both Jew and Gentile to-gether, we need to understand the problems we face from both sides of the *"wall of separation"* that divides us. Let's first look at the history of Israel so we, as Christians, can better understand.

Let's begin by looking at the birth, or introduction, of the law (the Torah) by reading what God says in Deuteronomy, one of the five books of Moses.

You shall therefore keep His statutes and His commandments which I command you today, that it may go well with you and with your chil-dren after you, and that you may prolong your days in the land which the LORD your God is giving you for all time.   (Deuteronomy 4:40)

Through these words of Moses, God told His children, the Jewish peo-ple, that they were to *"keep His statutes and His commandments."* Where confusion creeps in and divides us is due to *why* they were commanded to keep them. Look again: *"that it may go well with you and with your children after you."*

God isn't just giving His people useless rituals to perform. The law was not given by God in order to save or justify His people, but to give them directions on how to live so that their lives and the lives of their children would *"go well."*

> **The law was not given by God in order to save or justify His people, but to give them directions on how to live.**

As an illustration, it is like a parent telling their children to brush their teeth or eat their vegetables or not to play in the street. A father doesn't tell his child, "Brush your teeth so that I will love you more." A mother doesn't say, "Eat your vegetables and you'll get a bigger allowance." They would never say, "Don't play in the street and you'll get a new bike." That's preposterous. Parents have unconditional love for their children. Yet, we are told in God's Word that, as parents, we have a responsibility to *"Train up a child in the way he should go"* (Proverbs 22:6), and we are reminded that *"Foolishness is bound up in the heart of a child"* (verse 15).

Just yesterday Tiz and I took our Grandsugars (our grandchildren) to the Texas State Fair here in Dallas. They loved it. We gave them cotton candy, soda pop, and all kinds of junk food. Being only four years old, they don't understand that they can't live on such treats. After they arrived home, Anna, their mother and our eldest daughter, sat them down for dinner, but they didn't want what she had made for them. Their bellies were still full of cotton candy. Anna had to let them know that little boys shall not live by cotton candy alone. Eating green beans, brushing teeth, and avoiding the busy street aren't punishments or ways to earn love and rewards. They are simply wisdom. Why? So it may go well with them.

Tiz and I have been in the ministry for over thirty years. Many times, we have been asked, "Pastor Larry, do I need to tithe? I know it's a law, but doesn't the Bible say that we are not under the curse of the law?" As pastors, we can come off as confusing when we say things like, "We're not under the curse of the law, but don't forget that a tenth of everything is the Lord's."

Others will challenge me by saying, "Jesus didn't teach about tithing." But He did.

> *Woe to you, scribes and Pharisees, hypocrites! For you pay tithe of mint and anise and cummin, and have neglected the weightier matters of the law: justice and mercy and faith. These you ought to have done, without leaving the others undone.* (Matthew 23:23)

The reason Jesus didn't have to teach on tithing over and over again was because they were already doing it. He didn't have to spend time teaching what they already knew and obeyed. How did they know? Look again. They were *"matters of the law"*—the Torah, the pathway. Why did God make tithing a law? So it might go well for us and our children. Where did this law of tithing come from? To understand why God gave us this law, let's go back to the origins of tithing. It was not due to a law, but a revelation!

> *Now when Abram heard that his brother was taken captive, he armed his three hundred and eighteen trained servants who were born in his own house, and went in pursuit as far as Dan. He divided his forces against them by night, and he and his servants attacked them and pursued them as far as Hobah, which is north of Damascus. So he brought back all the goods, and also brought back his brother Lot and his goods, as well as the women and the people. And the king of Sodom went out to meet him at the Valley of Shaveh (that is, the King's Valley), after his return from the defeat of Chedorlaomer and the kings who were with him. Then Melchizedek king of Salem brought out bread and wine; he was the priest of God Most High. And he blessed him and said: "Blessed be Abram of God Most High, Possessor of heaven and earth; and blessed be God Most High, Who has delivered your enemies into your hand." And he gave him a tithe of all.* (Genesis 14:14–20)

Abram heard that Lot and others had been taken captive. So, he gathered a small gang of three hundred and eighteen trained servants and went after them. God gave Abram a miracle victory and he brought back Lot and all the goods. Then Abram met Melchizedek and gave him *"a tithe of all."*

> *Now consider how great this man was, to whom even the patriarch Abraham gave a tenth of the spoils. And indeed those who are of the*

sons of Levi, who receive the priesthood, have a commandment to re-
ceive tithes from the people according to the law, that is, from their breth-
ren, though they have come from the loins of Abraham; but he whose
genealogy is not derived from them received tithes from Abraham and
blessed him who had the promises. Now beyond all contradiction the
lesser is blessed by the better. Here mortal men receive tithes, but there
he receives them, of whom it is witnessed that he lives. Even Levi, who
receives tithes, paid tithes through Abraham, so to speak, for he was
still in the loins of his father when Melchizedek met him.

(Hebrews 7:4–10)

Here, in both the Old and New Testament, God teaches us about tith-ing, not as a law but, as Abram (Abraham) tithed, by revelation. There was no way Abram should have won that battle. He was out-manned and out-gunned. Yet Abram, before any law had been given, gave Melchizadek a tithe. Why? He had the revelation that his victory came only because of God. So why did God find the need to turn this revelation into law? *That it would go well with us and our children.*

You and I should know what to do but we sometimes get off the track, so God makes it plain, by His Word, what we can and cannot do. It's for our own good. If we want a harvest we must sow a seed. *"While the earth remains, seedtime and har-vest"* (Genesis 8:22). We know this. We know that if there is no seed, there will be no harvest. God says, "Do what I tell you. I love you. If you do what I say, it will be well with you."

> **We sometimes get off the track, so God makes it plain, by His Word, what we can and cannot do.**

As I'm writing this, I can't help but think about yesterday when Tiz and I were bringing the kids home from the fair. I saw a car stopped on the bridge with its flashers on and a bike lying in the road. My heart jumped into my throat. Then, I saw a lady frantically calling over the side of the bridge. Images—bad images—began to flash through my mind. As I slammed on the brakes and rushed out of the car, I yelled, "Is everything alright? Can I help you?" The woman turned to me, and with fear and anger in her eyes, said, "My son's in the creek fishing and I told him never go down there without his Dad or me." I then saw this little guy coming up out of the creek, head down and crying. I thought, *Oh boy, somebody's in trouble.*

Why was Mom so upset? Was it because she didn't want her son to go fishing? No, in fact I'd bet that if Mom and Dad had taken him fishing, they all would have been so happy if he would have caught the biggest fish of his life. She wasn't upset because he was fishing but because he was by himself. Like any loving parents, they had laid down the *law.* "You don't go fishing by yourself." The boy may not have understood all the dangers the creek held, but Mom and Dad did. So, they gave him rules to follow, not to earn their love, but because they already loved him so much that they knew their laws would keep him safe—and it would go well for him. As we drove off, I told Tiz, "Somebody's in trouble, probably going to get spanked." Then I thought about our heavenly Father. God *spanks,* or chastises, those He loves.

Let's get back to Israel. God delivered them from Egypt. He then gave Moses, a representative of His children, the Torah. For the sake of brevity, let's refer to the Torah as *the law.* The Ten Commandments is the *Reader's Digest,* or the condensed, version of all of God's laws. So the history of God's people goes like this: God delivers His people because He loves them; He gives them the law (the Ten Commandments) so they can be blessed; they forget about God and start living like Gentiles (nonbelievers); they get into trouble; they cry out to God again; He saves them again because He loves them as a parent loves a child; they begin to obey again and the blessings begin to flow; they forget about God again.... Well, you see the pattern.

Does that sound like anybody you know? Cry out, get saved, obey and be blessed, backslide and get into trouble, cry out again when the bottom falls out.

This time, Israel not only gets into trouble but is taken back into captivity, this time in Babylon.

Building a Fence

Here is where it really gets interesting. When the Jews finally left Babylon, the leaders of Israel called a meeting that became called the Great Assembly.

This was a group of Jewish leaders who were committed to finding a solution to Israel's problem of repeatedly forgetting about God's Word, thereby allowing their enemies an open door to defeat them. One of the leaders committed to protecting Israel and serving God was a scribe named Ezra.

> *For Ezra had prepared his heart to seek the Law of the LORD, and to do it, and to teach statutes and ordinances in Israel.*   (Ezra 7:10)

Ezra's heart was not only set on bringing Israel back to God, but also on putting them back on "the path"—the Torah—and to somehow keep them from falling away, getting lost, and living again like the Gentiles. So the Great Assembly came up with an idea: put a fence around God's law— the Torah—so that Israel would never again be able to wander near the edge of the path and fall off. It would be similar to putting a fence around your property.

> *Be prudent in judgment, raise up many disciples, and make a **fence** around the Torah.*
>   (Pirkei Avot 1:1/*Ethics of the Fathers*, emphasis added)

There was one problem with this strategy. When the fence is around God's Word, it not only keeps your children from getting out, but it also keeps your neighbor from getting in. Now, over two thousand years later, this fence has become part of the wall that divides us.

What's Our Problem?

Before I go any further in describing Israel's background, let's take a look at our part of the problem—the wall. As I just wrote the words, "our part of the problem," I felt the need to say that this is only *part* of our part of the problem, but it is a great place to start.

I want you to read a prophetic sermon by a great man of God, Rabbi Schneerson. It was not only a sermon or a message, but also a prophecy because: 1) his teachings came directly from God's Word; and 2) when he spoke them, those who heard them prophesied about this very book, *The Torah Blessing.* Isn't it exciting that God continues to speak to people all over the world? In his message, Rabbi Schneerson taught about the fulfillment of Isaiah's prophecy. Read with me about how the prophet speaks about you and me.

> *Thus says the Lord God: "Behold, I will lift My hand in an oath to the nations, and set up My standard for the peoples; they shall bring your sons in their arms, and your daughters shall be carried on their shoulders."* (Isaiah 49:22)

> *"And I will also take some of them for priests and Levites," says the Lord.* (Isaiah 66:21)

Unfortunately, Rabbi Schneerson passed away in 1994, but here were his words that day:

> How can a non-Jew have such spiritual power? Many Jews have abandoned the Torah to assimilate, to fit in with the world, to look like the Gentiles who do not follow the seven laws of Noah. So, as soon as the Gentiles come back to God's word, they will quickly lead the Jews, who have strayed, back to God. The world is ready for the Messiah. When the Gentile is seen keeping God's Word, the Jew will ask him, "Why do you do this?" And, the Jew will not be able to get this out of his mind. The Gentiles who come back to the seven Noahaic Laws, they will begin to keep the Sabbath, eat kosher, celebrate Rosh Hashanah, Yom Kippur, etc. Then every Jew will run to embrace God's word. The Gentiles themselves have no idea that they are ready. They have never heard of the seven Noahaic Laws but God will raise up among them teachers.

This teaching of Rabbi Schneerson is not only teaching us about the prophecy of Isaiah, but it is also the prophecy we get from Paul.

> *But I say, did Israel not know? First Moses says: "I will provoke you to jealousy by those who are not a nation, I will move you to anger by a foolish nation." But Isaiah is very bold and says: "I was found by those who did not seek Me; I was made manifest to those who did not ask for Me."* (Romans 10:19–20)

The word *provoke* is not a negative word but one that is positive. It means "to stimulate." Imagine the day when our Jewish brothers and sisters see the blessing of God on the Gentiles as we begin to understand the miracles in Shabbat, Rosh Hashanah, Yom Kippur, etc.—as we add to our faith in Jesus their knowledge of the Torah.

> *Till we all come to the unity of the faith and of the knowledge of the Son of God, to a perfect man, to the measure of the stature of the fullness of Christ.* (Ephesians 4:13)

When we do, the Jews will add to their knowledge, faith. Look again at what Rabbi Schneerson says: "The Gentiles, themselves have no idea that they are ready." Why is that? Why do most of us Gentiles have no idea that we are ready? We know the Scriptures, we know Jesus is about to return, and we know God said that He will rebuild the tabernacle of David. So what's our problem? What is holding us back?

It's simple; there is one word that scares us: "law." I would be willing to guess that out of that entire teaching by Rabbi Schneerson, there is one thing that stood out the most. It *should* have been when he said, "The world is ready for the Messiah," or "How can a non-Jew have such spiritual power?" or even, "God will raise up among them leaders." But I would guess that what caught your attention the most was when he said "laws," or more specifically, "the seven Noahaic Laws." You may think, *But Larry, I've never heard of these laws.* But you have, but we don't call them that.

> *And with this the words of the prophets agree, just as it is written: "After this I will return and will rebuild the tabernacle of David, which has fallen down; I will rebuild its ruins, and I will set it up; so that the rest of mankind may seek the* Lord, *even all the Gentiles who are called by My name, says the* Lord *who does all these things." Known to God from eternity are all His works. Therefore I judge that we should not trouble those from among the Gentiles who are turning to God, but that we write to them to abstain from things polluted by idols, from sexual immorality, from things strangled, and from blood. For Moses has had throughout many generations those who preach him in every city, being read in the synagogues every Sabbath.* (Acts 15:15–21)

I've already mentioned this, but let me quickly review it with you. This, in Acts 15, is called the Jerusalem Council. Leaders of the first church were meeting to discuss what to teach all the new converts because they many were Gentiles and had no idea how to serve God. This first move of God to graft the Gentiles into Israel (see Romans 16:17) was the first step in the prophecy of rebuilding the tabernacle of David. (See Acts 15:16–17.) James was saying, in effect, "Let's not give them too much, but start them out with what God has given us to tell all Gentiles." (See Acts 15:20.) Those five teachings were the basics of the law that God gave everybody—the milk of the Word. Then, in the next verse, James suggests that these new converts will go back to their cities and grow as they hear God's Word. How? The words and exploits of Moses were being taught in the synagogues every Sabbath.

> **Why are we so nervous about the word *law*? Because man—not God—has confused us!**

Why are we so nervous about the word *law*? Because man—not God—has confused us! Where does this confusion come from? Look at what Paul says.

> For God is not the author of confusion but of peace, as in all the churches of the saints. (1 Corinthians 14:33)

Confusion: From Man or God?

Let's look at a few Scriptures that we've all read and heard, but which have often brought about confusion.

> The law of the LORD is perfect, converting the soul; the testimony of the LORD is sure, making wise the simple. (Psalm 19:7)

The Law of the Lord is perfect. The statutes of the Lord are right.

> Blessed are the undefiled in the way, who walk in the law of the LORD! (Psalm 119:1)

> For as many as are of the works of the law are under the curse; for it is written, "Cursed is everyone who does not continue in all things which are written in the book of the law, to do them." (Galatians 3:10)

Those under the *law* are also under a *curse*.

For sin shall not have dominion over you, for you are not under law but under grace. What then? Shall we sin because we are not under law but under grace? Certainly not! (Romans 6:14–15)

Confusing, isn't it? At one point, God's Word seems to say that those who walk in the law are blessed, but then, it *seems* to contradict itself by saying that whoever walks in the law is also under a curse. Then, consider these Scriptures:

For by grace you have been saved through faith, and that not of yourselves; it is the gift of God, not of works, lest anyone should boast. (Ephesians 2:8–9)

Therefore, my beloved, as you have always obeyed, not as in my presence only, but now much more in my absence, work out your own salvation with fear and trembling. (Philippians 2:12)

On one hand, Paul tells us that we are saved by grace but then he tells us to "*work out*" our salvation. It seems to get even more confusing.

Is the law then against the promises of God? Certainly not! For if there had been a law given which could have given life, truly righteousness would have been by the law. (Galatians 3:21)

What shall we say then? Is the law sin? Certainly not! On the contrary, I would not have known sin except through the law. For I would not have known covetousness unless the law had said, "You shall not covet." (Romans 7:7)

Remember, it is the truth you *understand* that will set you free. Here is the key that will unlock God's Word for you. In Greek, the word for *law* is almost always translated from the word *nomos*. Even though it is always translated as *law* in the New Testament, it doesn't always mean the same thing.

*Do not think that I came to destroy **the Law** or the Prophets. I did not come to destroy but to fulfill. For assuredly, I say to you, till heaven and earth pass away, one jot or one tittle will by no means pass from the law till all is fulfilled.* (Matthew 5:17–18, emphasis added)

Jesus said that He didn't come to do away with the law (*nomos*) but to show us, even give us, the ability to live it. Now, read about Paul's teaching of being under the curse of the law.

> *For sin shall not have dominion over you, for you are not under **law** but under grace. What then? Shall we sin because we are not under **law** but under grace? Certainly not!* (Romans 6:14–15, emphasis added)

Here we have the word *law* (*nomos*) again, but this time it is a curse. Why? In the time of Jesus and Paul, there was no word in Greek for "legalism." Legalism is what Jesus is talking about in Matthew.

> *For they bind heavy burdens, hard to bear, and lay them on men's shoulders; but they themselves will not move them with one of their fingers.* (Matthew 23:4)

David Stern, a friend who wrote *The Jewish New Testament Commentary*, tells us that when Paul used the term *"under the law"* (*upo nomon*) it means "man-made" law (legalism), not "God-made" law (Torah).

Back to the Great Assembly

Remember when God's children came out of Babylon and their leaders gathered together to come up with a plan to stop the negative, backsliding pattern of Israelites? Inevitably, Israel would fall into trouble, and God would have to come to their rescue. Grateful, they would serve the Lord, and His blessings would flow. Eventually, they would forget the Lord again and start living like the Gentiles (non-Jews), allowing their enemies to defeat them again. The Great Assembly wrestled with how to keep Israel from forgetting the teachings of God? Their solution was to erect a "fence" around God's Word. In the oral Torah, this fence was called the *mishnah*. These were man-made boundaries or laws.

In all fairness, man-made fences or boundaries are not always bad. For example, we all know what God's Word says about adultery—it's wrong, right? So, most churches put up a fence—a boundary—so that God's children don't fall off the path. They make rules that a staff member is not to council someone of the opposite sex alone or with the door closed. Such rules are not a bad idea; in fact, they are a good idea. Such rules are part of a man-made fence that keeps God's children from stumbling and falling off the path. It begins to go wrong is when we take man's laws and make them equal with God's law. When that happens, laws go from a good idea to a curse.

We have all probably seen churches or entire denominations use man-made laws to put people under a curse. Man's laws have declared that women are not allowed to put on make-up or wear pants. Man's laws have outlawed movies, television, dancing, singing, and the playing of musical instruments. I'm sure that many of you are adding things from your experience to this list—things that you were taught that came from man's word, not God's Word, things that became "law" in your church or denomination. Praise God, the *truth you know (now) has set you free.* Remember, God gave His Torah—His laws or commandments—not to bind man up but "*that it may go well with you*" (Deuteronomy 4:40). But, it got to the point that those fences—the oral laws—took on as much, if not more, authority than God's Word.

What I'm about to explain may just change the way you read God's Word and, as a result, change your life. Look with me at Jesus' teaching in the book of Mark.

> *Then the Pharisees and some of the scribes came together to Him, having come from Jerusalem. Now when they saw some of His disciples eat bread with defiled, that is, with unwashed hands, they found fault. For the Pharisees and all the Jews do not eat unless they wash their hands in a special way, holding the tradition of the elders. When they come from the marketplace, they do not eat unless they wash. And there are many other things which they have received and hold, like the washing of cups, pitchers, copper vessels, and couches. Then the Pharisees and scribes asked Him, "Why do Your disciples not walk according to the tradition of the elders, but eat bread with unwashed hands?" He answered and said to them, "Well did Isaiah prophesy of you hypocrites, as it is written: 'This people honors Me with their lips, but their heart is far from Me. And in vain they worship Me, teaching as doctrines the commandments of men.' For laying aside the commandment of God, you hold the tradition of men; the washing of pitchers and cups, and many other such things you do." He said to them, "All too well you reject the*

commandment of God, that you may keep your tradition...making the word of God of no effect through your tradition which you have handed down. And many such things you do." (Mark 7:1–9, 13)

Some of the religious people came to Jesus because they were upset. They had seen some of Jesus' disciples eating their bread with what they considered to be defiled, unwashed hands. Once again remember, God gave us the Torah—the law—*"that it may go well with you."* God gave us laws so that He could bless us and keep us safe. One of the laws in the Torah is about washing your hands before you eat. Why? Also remember, everything God teaches us has two parts—spiritual and physical. Let's look first at the spiritual part of God's law concerning the washing of your hands before you eat.

In Judaism, one of the worst things you can do is take God's blessing for granted. So before you begin to eat, everyone bows their head and gives thanks over the meal. Originally, this was combined with not only the breaking of bread, but also with the washing of hands, pausing to give God thanks. Today, we rush through our meals so fast that many of God's children barely even slow down to thank the Lord for His provision in our lives. That's the spiritual part in a nutshell.

But there is also the physical part. When the Lord first commanded His children to wash their hands, they didn't understand about germs, disease, and sickness—but God did. Now, you may think, *But, Larry, we're not under the law.* Maybe not, but I'm sure glad that the restaurant employees who make my pizzas are "under the law." When you go into the restroom in any restaurant, there is always a sign reminding employees that the law requires that they wash their hands before returning to work. I say, "Thank God!" Shout grace all you want, I still want God's law: wash your hands.

But this is not what Jesus is dealing with in Mark. The elders came to Jesus because His disciples ate bread with defiled hands. Were the disciples defiled in God's eyes or man's eyes? Did they break God's law of washing, or man's law of washing? In verse 3, it suggests that the elders didn't just want his followers to wash their hands, but to do so *"in a special way, holding the tradition of the elders."*

Look at verse 5. The elders didn't ask Jesus, "Why didn't your disciples wash according to the word of God?" They asked, *"Why do Your disciples not walk according to the tradition of the elders?"* Why aren't they following the rules of the Great Assembly? Why are they ignoring the "fence"—the man-made laws? Now, notice what Jesus told them. He said, in effect, "You hypocrites! You are not honoring Me. You are teaching the doctrines of men." In other words, you are taking man-made laws and teaching them as if they were the words of God.

Let me give you a great example of this. What you are about to read is a section of the Talmud (the oral Torah). Here, you get a clear glimpse of how man-made rules can go far beyond God's teachings.

> If a man poured water over one hand with a single rinsing, his hand is clean; but if over both hands with a single rinsing, Rabbi Meir, declares them unclean unless he pours over them a quarter log or more. If a loaf of heave offering fell [on the water] it remains clean, but Rabbi Jose declares it unclean.
>
> If he pours the first water over one place and the second water over another, and the loaf of heave offering fell on the first water, it becomes unclean. If he poured both the first water and the second over the same place and the loaf of the heave offering fell there on, it becomes unclean. If he poured the first water [over his hands] and a piece of wood or gravel was found on his hands, his hands remain unclean...   (taken from Yadin section of the Mishnah)

Are they serious? God said, in effect, "Wash your hands. You may not understand why, but do it, *'that it may go well with you.'"* Man turned this into a burden-riddled obligation. Now, we can understand why Jesus rebuked those teachers who taught man's law as if it was God's law.

> *For they bind heavy burdens, hard to bear, and lay them on men's shoulders; but they themselves will not move them with one of their fingers.*   (Matthew 23:4)

Man's law—the fence—binds men up with burdens no one can manage.

> *But woe to you, scribes and Pharisees, hypocrites! For you shut up the kingdom of heaven against men; for you neither go in yourselves, nor do you allow those who are entering to go in.*   (verse 13)

Jesus said that they had *"shut up the kingdom of heaven."* Nobody can follow such man-made laws. We can't even understand them, much less do them. Let's go back to Jesus' teaching on tithing:

> *Woe to you, scribes and Pharisees, hypocrites! For you pay tithe of mint and anise and cummin, and have neglected the weightier matters of the law: justice and mercy and faith. These you ought to have done, without leaving the others undone. Blind guides, who strain out a gnat and swallow a camel!*   (Matthew 23:23–24)

Jesus rebuked them again for straining at a gnat but swallowing a camel. He was saying that, yes, tithing is part of God's law, but then He pointed out that there are things that God's Word teaches us that are even more important. God instructs us to wash our hands, not to bind us up with heavy, confusing burdens, but that it may go well with us. Who is able to wash their hands in the way these man-made laws teach? Jesus described the joy of God's law: *"My yoke is easy and My burden is light"* (Matthew 11:30). Compare that to man's religious traditions that *"bind heavy burdens, hard to bear, and lay them on men's shoulders"* (Matthew 23:4).

> *But you, do not be called "Rabbi"; for One is your Teacher, the Christ, and you are all brethren.*   (verse 8)

By teaching man's rules, the elders were actually laying aside the commandments of God so they could uphold the traditions of men. Jesus went on to say that it was not just about washing hands, but included many of the other things they did, as well.

Because of religious traditions, it's possible that we can actually *reject* God's Word, *"making the word of God of no effect through your tradition which you have handed down. And many such things you do"* (Mark 7:13).

Many of you have probably experienced exactly what Jesus was dealing with two thousand years ago. God gave you a promise that His yoke would be light, that He would not burden you with all the religious dos and don'ts *"that it may go well with you."* It wasn't long, however, before the man's tradition weighed you down and *canceled out* the blessings that God intended for you. God gave us the Sabbath as a great gift—intended for joy, blessing, and peace. It is a time for God and for family. Yet even in

Jesus' day, religious traditions tried to make God's blessing *"of no effect"* by losing its real meaning.

> *Now it happened that He went through the grainfields on the Sabbath; and as they went His disciples began to pluck the heads of grain. And the Pharisees said to Him, "Look, why do they do what is not lawful on the Sabbath?" But He said to them, "Have you never read what David did when he was in need and hungry, he and those with him: how he went into the house of God in the days of Abiathar the high priest, and ate the showbread, which is not lawful to eat, except for the priests, and also gave some to those who were with him?" And He said to them, "The Sabbath was made for man, and not man for the Sabbath. Therefore the Son of Man is also Lord of the Sabbath."*
>
> (Mark 2:23–28)

I love what Jesus said here. God gave us the Sabbath because *"the Sabbath was made for man."* Religion says, "Don't do this and don't do that on the Sabbath." It takes away the blessing. It is so important that we understand the difference between God's Word that leads us, guides us, and blesses us, and man's tradition that binds us up with heavy burdens. (See Matthew 23:4.) Let's look at a few more examples.

> *Then the scribes and Pharisees who were from Jerusalem came to Jesus, saying, "Why do Your disciples transgress the tradition of the elders? For they do not wash their hands when they eat bread." He answered and said to them, "Why do you also transgress the commandment of God because of your tradition?"* (Matthew 15:1–3)

Look closely at what is going on in this passage. The scribes and Pharisees told Jesus that His disciples violated *"the tradition of the elders."* They were not accused of violating the Word of God, but the *fence* around the Torah that the elders had constructed. Jesus came right back at them, *"Why do you also transgress the commandment of God?"* How were they transgressing against God? They were doing so with their burdensome *tradition*.

> *Beware lest anyone cheat you through philosophy and empty deceit, according to the tradition of men, according to the basic principles of the world, and not according to Christ.* (Colossians 2:8)

Paul warned us to watch out for those who would cheat us. He then told us who it was we should watch out for: *"the world"* and *"the tradition of men."* You've probably been warned before of the need to be aware of what the world teaches that is contrary to God's Word, but Paul included man's religious traditions in the same warning.

> *Therefore rebuke them sharply, that they may be sound in the faith, not giving heed to Jewish fables and commandments of men who turn from the truth.* (Titus 1:14–15)

Here we have a letter from the apostle Paul to Titus warning him that they should not to listen to Jewish fables or to the commandments of men. *"You shall not steal"* (Exodus 20:8) is not a Jewish fable, nor is it man's commandment. It is a commandment straight from God. The same is true for all of the Ten Commandments. The same is true with remembering the Sabbath, and with washing your hands before you make my pizza. (Please!) These truths only become Jewish—and Christian—fables when we add man-made rules, or *fences*, around them and pretend that they came from God. One of the greatest teachings concerning this is found in the book of Acts.

> *Now therefore, why do you test God by putting a yoke on the neck of the disciples which neither our fathers nor we were able to bear?* (Acts 15:10)

Once again, this was the Jerusalem Council where Paul, Barnabas, Peter, and other leaders of the first century church were meeting. Their purpose was to discuss what to do with all the new Gentile converts who were receiving Jesus as their savior. Many of the Jewish leaders wanted to go back to the old ways, but Peter's reply, in the verse above, asked, "How can we put a yoke on them that neither we nor our fathers could possibly bear?" Remember the burdensome description of proper hand washing from earlier in this chapter? That is not the law (*nomos*)—the Torah of God. That is being under the law (*upo nomon*). To this, Paul said that we are not under the curse of the law.

> *For as many as are of the works of the law are under the curse; for it is written, "Cursed is everyone who does not continue in all things which are written in the book of the law, to do them."* (Galatians 3:10)

Do not think that I came to destroy the Law or the Prophets. I did not come to destroy but to fulfill. (Matthew 5:17)

Jesus didn't come to stop us from washing our hands, but to break the curse of man's traditions. He said, in effect, "I didn't come to take away the Sabbath, but if I'm hungry on the Sabbath, I'm going to eat. I didn't come to destroy the Law or the Prophets, but to show you how to walk with God's Word, not the traditions of men, so that it may go well with you and your children who come after you."

Therefore the law is holy, and the commandment holy and just and good. (Romans 7:12)

God's law is *"holy and just and good"*!

Fiddler on the Roof

One of my favorite Broadway musicals and movies is the old classic, *Fiddler on the Roof*. In fact, my cell phone ringtone is the opening song, "Tradition." That's where the show got its name. In the story, Tevye, the father, says, "Life is like a fiddler on the roof; it's hard to keep playing and keep your balance at the same time, the balance between life, family, God, and traditions."

If you've ever seen it, you may remember the scene where Tevye went to meet with Lazar Wolf, the butcher. They agreed that Lazar would marry Tevye's daughter, Tzeitel. To celebrate their agreement, the two men went to the local tavern. Inside, the tavern was divided, not by a visible, physical wall, but by an invisible separation—tradition. On one side were the Jews. On the other side were the non-Jews, in this case Russian Gentile Christians. All the Jewish men were singing and dancing in celebration of the upcoming marriage of Tzeitel and Lazar Wolf. They were having a great time laughing and singing when something surprising happened. Hearing of Tevye's good fortune, one of the Gentiles reached out his hand to Tevye to offer congratulations. Without thinking, Tevye began to reach his hand out as well when he suddenly realized what he was doing, stopped, and instantly pulled his had back. Why would he refuse this offer of good will? This Russian was not a stranger; they all lived together in a small village. Why, then, did Tevye hesitate to touch this Gentile?

Let's go back to Ezra and the Great Assembly after Israel came back from Babylon. Their main concerns were: 1) "How do we keep from falling away from God?" and 2) "How do we keep from becoming like the Gentiles, idol worshippers?" God's Word said, *"You shall have no other gods before Me"* (Exodus 20:3). But the Great Assembly put a *fence* around the Torah. It was true that God did not want them to act like Gentiles by worshipping idols or other gods. Thus, the *fence*—the man-made tradition—dictated that Jews were forbidden to even *touch* a Gentile! This was the reason Tevye pulled his hand back. God said, "Don't act like the world." Man's tradition says, "To ensure you don't act like them, you won't be allowed even to touch them."

Here is another one of my favorite teachings of Jesus:

> *You are the salt of the earth; but if the salt loses its flavor, how shall it be seasoned? It is then good for nothing but to be thrown out and trampled underfoot by men. You are the light of the world. A city that is set on a hill cannot be hidden. Nor do they light a lamp and put it under a basket, but on a lampstand, and it gives light to all who are in the house. Let your light so shine before men, that they may see your good works and glorify your Father in heaven.* (Matthew 5:13–16)

This is from Jesus' Sermon on the Mount, one of the most famous Scriptures in all of Christianity. Jesus was teaching that we are the light of the world. This is a very powerful statement. "You...you...are the *light* of the world." Who was Jesus talking to when He said, "You"? Most would say that he was talking about us—the church. He was calling us to be the light of the world. There is only one problem with that: at that time, there was no "us", and there was no church. Sure, now, we have been grafted in, and we have that calling, but when Jesus spoke those words by the Sea of Galilee, he had a different audience. His was not speaking to Christians but to Jews.

> *Great multitudes followed Him; from Galilee, and from Decapolis, Jerusalem, Judea, and beyond the Jordan. And seeing the multitudes,*

He went up on a mountain, and when He was seated His disciples
came to Him. (Matthew 4:25–5:1)

Jesus told them, in effect, "God didn't call you to be the light to the
world that you would hide your light under a basket!" In the Torah, there
are many commandments that God gave to Israel. Among them was God's
encouragement to Israel, saying, "Don't keep this to yourself. Share *Me* and
My Word with the world—the Gentiles—so that they can know Me, too!"

Therefore be careful to observe them; for this is your wisdom and your
understanding in the sight of the peoples who will hear all these statutes,
and say, "Surely this great nation is a wise and understanding people.
For what great nation is there that has God so near to it, as the Lord
our God is to us, for whatever reason we may call upon Him?
(Deuteronomy 4:6–7)

God said, "Keep the Torah," and the nations of the world—Gentile
nations—will say, "What other great nations are there that have a God so
near to them as God is to Israel whenever they call on Him?" Another one
of my favorite Scriptures is the prophecy that one day Gentiles would come
to the God of Abraham, Isaac, and Jacob.

O Lord, *my strength and my fortress, my refuge in the day of afflic-*
tion, the Gentiles shall come to You from the ends of the earth and
say, "Surely our fathers have inherited lies, worthlessness and unprofit-
able things." Will a man make gods for himself, which are not gods?
"Therefore behold, I will this once cause them to know, I will cause
them to know My hand and My might; and they shall know that My
name is the Lord." (Jeremiah 16:19–21)

Thus says the Lord *of hosts: "In those days ten men from every lan-*
guage of the nations shall grasp the sleeve of a Jewish man, saying, 'Let
us go with you, for we have heard that God is with you.'"
(Zechariah 8:23)

This is why, when that Russian Gentile extended his hand, Tevye pulled
his hand back. Man's tradition says, "Don't be like the Gentiles—don't

even touch them." This is what Peter faced when he experienced a vision on a rooftop.

> *The next day, as they went on their journey and drew near the city, Peter went up on the housetop to pray, about the sixth hour. Then he became very hungry and wanted to eat; but while they made ready, he fell into a trance and saw heaven opened and an object like a great sheet bound at the four corners, descending to him and let down to the earth. In it were all kinds of four-footed animals of the earth, wild beasts, creeping things, and birds of the air. And a voice came to him, "Rise, Peter; kill and eat." But Peter said, "Not so, Lord! For I have never eaten anything common or unclean." And a voice spoke to him again the second time, "What God has cleansed you must not call common."*
>
> (Acts 10:9–15)

You've probably heard this story before, but do you understand it? Before Peter's rooftop experience, Cornelius, a Gentile, was praying when he had a vision of his own.

> *There was a certain man in Caesarea called Cornelius, a centurion of what was called the Italian Regiment, a devout man and one who feared God with all his household, who gave alms generously to the people, and prayed to God always. About the ninth hour of the day he saw clearly in a vision an angel of God coming in and saying to him, "Cornelius!"*
>
> (Acts 10:1–3)

In this vision, God told Cornelius to send men to Joppa to get a man named Peter. Here's the problem: God told Cornelius—a Gentile, a non-Jew—to go and find Peter—a Jew—and invite him into his home. There was no way that Peter would accept the invitation because to a Jew, Cornelius was "unclean." Even though God's Word said Jews were to be a light to the world—to Gentiles—man's tradition had built a *fence*, a wall that divided Jew from Gentile. Jews were forbidden to touch, eat with, or fellowship with the "unclean." So, God sent Peter a vision that said, in effect, "When I call something clean, don't you dare call it unclean." Having seen the vision, Peter went to see Cornelius.

Then he said to them, "You know how unlawful it is for a Jewish man to keep company with or go to one of another nation. But God has shown me that I should not call any man common or unclean.

(Acts 10:28)

Peter was obeying God's word, not man's traditions. You may know the rest of the story. In verse 34, Peter said, *"In truth I perceive that God shows no partiality."* Later, as Peter was speaking, the Holy Spirit fell on everyone.

While Peter was still speaking these words, the Holy Spirit fell upon all those who heard the word. (Acts 10:44)

Look out! That could mean trouble. Sure enough, read what happened next:

Now the apostles and brethren who were in Judea heard that the Gentiles had also received the word of God. And when Peter came up to Jerusalem, those of the circumcision contended with him, saying, "You went in to uncircumcised men and ate with them!"

(Acts 11:1–3)

The fence, that wall of division, was beginning to crumble.

In closing, let me say this: It's not just the traditions of man that have built up the wall that has divided Jew and Gentile. Over the centuries, the Christian church has done many shameful and hurtful things to the Jewish people and to Israel for which we need to repent. Indeed, the wall that divides has been built from the teachings of men— both on the Jewish side and on the Christian side. It's time to stop letting man *"bind heavy burdens, hard to bear, and lay them on men's shoulders"* (Matthew 23:4). It is time for the truth you know to *"make you free"!* (John 8:32) When Jesus and Paul taught us about the law—the Torah, the path—it was not to be legalistic, but *"that it may go well"* (Deuteronomy 4:40) with us and our children. When Jesus and Paul spoke about the

> **The wall that divides has been built from the teachings of men—both on the Jewish side and on the Christian side.**

heavy burden of man's traditions or being under the curse of the law, they were referring to the *fence*, man-made fables that make God's Word *"of no effect"* (Mark 7:13) so that nobody wants it.

I feel in my spirit that I need to tell you about a Jewish man I met at the Dead Sea in Israel. Tiz and I were leading a tour to Israel. As our group was checking into their rooms at the hotel, I grabbed Tiz and the kids and we ran down to the water. My children had never been in the Dead Sea before, and they were having a great time. We were all laughing and splashing about when I noticed a man and his wife watching us. She was sitting in a chair on the shore, and he was standing in the water not far from her. As we continued to swim and play, he came out to where we were. With a smile on his face, he asked, "Is this your family?" I told him that it was and that this was their first time in Israel. As we talked, I could tell there was something on his mind.

Finally, he said to me, "Can I ask you a question?"

"Sure," I said.

"Around your neck, is that a Star of David, a 'Mogan David'?"

"Yes," I answered.

"And a cross?" he asked.

"Yes."

"How can that be?" he asked. "A Star of David *and* a cross?"

I told him about the things I have been sharing with you in this book. I explained how Jesus came to graft us—His followers—into Israel. I told him that Jesus didn't come to do away with the law, but to rescue us from being under man's curse, and to teach us how to walk on God's path.

Tears began to fill the man's eyes, and he said to me, "I'm an old man, and I'm looking for God. I don't want to wear black and be bound up by so many laws, but neither can I do what I see most Christians do. *This* is the God I'm looking for!"

My prayer is that what I've shown you in this chapter will fill in the missing piece of the puzzle—a piece the church has been in search of for two thousand years. God's Word does not put us under the curse of the law. Man-made traditions do that. In the book of Romans, Paul quoted Moses:

Brethren, my heart's desire and prayer to God for Israel is that they may be saved. For I bear them witness that they have a zeal for God, but not according to knowledge. For they being ignorant of God's righteousness, and seeking to establish their own righteousness, have not submitted to the righteousness of God. For Christ is the end of the law for righteousness to everyone who believes. For Moses writes about the righteousness which is of the law, "The man who does those things shall live by them." But the righteousness of faith speaks in this way, "Do not say in your heart, 'Who will ascend into heaven?'" (that is, to bring Christ down from above) or, "'Who will descend into the abyss?'" (that is, to bring Christ up from the dead). But what does it say? "The word is near you, in your mouth and in your heart" (that is, the word of faith which we preach): that if you confess with your mouth the Lord Jesus and believe in your heart that God has raised Him from the dead, you will be saved. For with the heart one believes unto righteousness, and with the mouth confession is made unto salvation. For the Scripture says, "Whoever believes on Him will not be put to shame." For there is no distinction between Jew and Greek, for the same Lord over all is rich to all who call upon Him. For "whoever calls on the name of the LORD *shall be saved." How then shall they call on Him in whom they have not believed? And how shall they believe in Him of whom they have not heard? And how shall they hear without a preacher? And how shall they preach unless they are sent? As it is written: "How beautiful are the feet of those who preach the gospel of peace, who bring glad tidings of good things!" But they have not all obeyed the gospel. For Isaiah says, "Lord, who has believed our report?" So then faith comes by hearing, and hearing by the word of God. But I say, have they not heard? Yes indeed: "Their sound has gone out to all the earth, and their words to the ends of the world." But I say, did Israel not know? First Moses says: "I will provoke you to jealousy by those who are not a nation, I will move you to anger by a foolish nation." But Isaiah is very bold and says: "I was found by those who did not seek Me; I was made manifest to those who did not ask for Me." But to Israel he says: "All day long I have stretched out My hands to a disobedient and contrary people."*

(Romans 10)

> **God's Word is not legalism; it's a path that you get to walk on.**

Do you know what Moses and Paul are saying to us? Now that you and I are saved by grace, not by works, God has provided a great path for us to walk on. *The man who does these things finds life!!!* When you tithe, you find life; when you find Shabbat, you find life; when you love your neighbor, you find life; when you wash your hands, you kill germs and find life. God's Word is not legalism; it's a path that you get to walk on *"that it may go well with you and with your children after you"* (Deuteronomy 4:40).

In the following chapters, I'm going to share with you a few of the things the Lord has taught me since that incredible first trip to Israel. You will learn about wearing the tallit, keeping the Sabbath, and celebrating the God-ordained feasts of Passover, Rosh Hashanah, Yom Kippur, Pentecost, and Sukkot. These are practices that have set Tiz and me—our family, our church, and our ministry—on an incredible path of worship, service, understanding, and miraculous blessing.

5

The Tallit (Prayer Shawl):
Healing in His Wings

*"Listen! Behold, a sower went out to sow. And it happened, as he
sowed, that some seed fell by the wayside; and the birds of the air came
and devoured it. Some fell on stony ground, where it did not have much
earth; and immediately it sprang up because it had no depth of earth.
But when the sun was up it was scorched, and because it had no root it
withered away. And some seed fell among thorns; and the thorns grew
up and choked it, and it yielded no crop. But other seed fell on good
ground and yielded a crop that sprang up, increased and produced:
some thirtyfold, some sixty, and some a hundred." And He said to
them, "He who has ears to hear, let him hear!"* (Mark 4:3–9)

This is the well-known parable of the seed and the sower. In it, Jesus
was talking about seed falling on various types of soil. Then, all
of a sudden, in verse nine, He declared, *"He who has ears to hear,
let him hear!"* Obviously, Jesus was not addressing people who were actually
missing ears on their heads. No, He was talking about people who heard
the words He spoke but had no ability to understand. He was saying, in
effect, "He who is anointed—touched and gifted by God with discernment
and understanding—let him understand."

Can't you just see the apostles standing behind Him, nodding in agreement? Then, in the next verse: *"When He was alone, those around Him with
the twelve asked Him about the parable"* (verse 10). His own disciples had no
understanding. Jesus then said to them, *"To you it has been given to know
the mystery of the kingdom of God; but to those who are outside, all things come*

in parables" (Mark 4:11). In other words, "To you who are born again, I am going to explain the mysteries of the kingdom of God, but to everyone else, these teachings are merely going to be stories."

Until we read and understand Scripture through Jesus' eyes—the eyes of Yeshua the Messiah—and receive understanding by the Holy Spirit— the Spirit of the God of Abraham—the meaning of these teachings will remained locked in a neat little story. Let's ask God to help us go beyond the story to the place where the mystery of God's Word is revealed.

If Only I May Touch His Garment...

The following story of healing is found in three of the four Gospels.

> *Now a certain woman had a flow of blood for twelve years, and had suffered many things from many physicians. She had spent all that she had and was no better, but rather grew worse.* (Mark 5:25–26)

Here was a woman who suffered from a blood issue for twelve years. She had spent all of her money seeing every doctor and healer possible, but she could not get any better. She was about to try something that would prove she was at the end of her rope.

> *For she said to herself, "If only I may touch His garment, I shall be made well."* (Matthew 9:21)

Without going into graphic detail, let me just state that according to the Torah, a woman suffering from a flow of blood was considered to be "unclean." She was forbidden from appearing in public because anyone she touched was also viewed as unclean. Certainly, for such a woman to touch a rabbi was strictly forbidden. She had seen every doctor and had found no answer to her misery, but suddenly, she heard Jesus was coming. Imagine the desperation of this woman to enter a crowded public market full of witnesses in order to touch this visiting rabbi!

Perhaps you can relate to this woman. You don't feel worthy to go before a holy God, but you're desperate. You've tried everything, but you can't get your prosperity released, your debt cancelled, your kids serving God, or your husband to go to church. You can't find release from the bonds of sickness or addiction. You're sick and tired of being sick and tired. You've tried everything, and you're at the place where you are willing to try anything. You are desperate to find healing and wholeness.

This woman thought, *If I can just touch the hem of His garment, my years of suffering and torment will be over.* The word for *hem* is *kraspedon*, meaning "a tassel of twisted wool." This woman wasn't even trying to touch the cloth of Jesus' garments, only the tassel of wool that hung off the side of His prayer shawl.

The Tallit

In the Old Testament, there is a brief command: *"You shall make tassels on the four corners of the clothing with which you cover yourself"* (Deuteronomy 22:12). This is a strange little commandment in the middle of the chapter instructing the men of Israel in what to wear. No more explanation is given. It is preceded and followed by other aspects of Mosaic law. In Numbers, however, the command is expanded:

> *Again the LORD spoke to Moses, saying, "Speak to the children of Israel: tell them to make tassels on the corners of their garments throughout their generations, and to put a blue thread in the tassels of the corners. And you shall have the tassel, that you may look upon it and remember all the commandments of the LORD and do them."*
> (Numbers 15:37–39)

Therefore, "*throughout their generations,*" Jewish men were instantly recognizable by the tassels of twisted wool on the fringe of their outer garment. Jesus was no different.

Switching now to Luke's description of the woman's plight, the story continues as she "*came from behind and touched the border of His garment. And immediately her flow of blood stopped*" (Luke 8:44).

The traditional Jewish shawl with tassels on the four corners is called the *tallit*. The woven tassels represent the 613 commandments, or mitzvahs, of God that protect, lead, guide, and teach His people. Jesus, as a Jewish man who was called "Rabbi," would certainly have worn such a shawl. The

English translation of the edge of the tallit is *border*, but in Hebrew, it is also referred to as the *arba kanfot*, or "four wings."

Imagine this woman, who had grown up hearing stories of a coming Messiah. She had heard men speaking of the prophecies in Isaiah about one who was *"wounded for our transgressions, He was bruised for our iniquities; the chastisement for our peace was upon Him, and by His stripes we are healed"* (Isaiah 53:5). When she saw Jesus wearing the prayer shawl, she knew by God's promises that she would finally receive the miracle she had been seeking for so long. She had heard the prophecy that said, *"The Sun of Righteousness shall arise with healing in His wings"* (Malachi 4:2). She didn't try to brush his sleeve. She didn't cry out from afar. She knew the prophecy and had faith that God would be true to His Word, so she reached out and grabbed it. I'm sure it wasn't much. She'd suffered from bleeding for *twelve years!* She was probably sickly, thin, and weak in her appearance. Yet she reached out and grabbed that promise of God as it passed by her. And Jesus immediately stopped.

> *Jesus said, "Who touched Me?" When all denied it, Peter and those with him said, "Master, the multitudes throng and press You, and You say, 'Who touched Me?'" But Jesus said, "Somebody touched Me, for I perceived power going out from Me."* (Luke 8:45–46)

She touched the hem of the tallit, and Jesus *felt* the power go out. I don't know about you, but I would like to get in on some of that power.

> *Now when the woman saw that she was not hidden, she came trembling; and falling down before Him, she declared to Him in the presence of all the people the reason she had touched Him and how she was healed immediately. And He said to her, "Daughter, be of good cheer; your faith has made you well. Go in peace."* (verses 47–48)

Jesus didn't know this woman. He had never met her, but she knew that the Messiah would come—that Jesus would come—with healing in His wings.

Is it so preposterous to believe that by obeying God's Word and wearing a reminder of His promises when we pray, He will bring healing in the wings of the tallit? You might think, *Why would we need something so external in order to facilitate God's healing?*

Is it true that when we anoint people with oil, they will be healed? (See, for example, James 5:14.)

Is it true that when we lay hands on the sick, they will recover? (See, for example, Mark 16:18.)

Is it true that we should put guards on our mouths, for there is life and death in the power of the tongue? (See Proverbs 18:21.)

Is there any use in rejoicing in the Lord always, for God inhabits the praises of his people? (See Psalm 22:3; Philippians 4:4.)

Is it true that our tithes and offerings will open up the windows of heaven? (See Malachi 3:10.)

Is it true that when we sing and praise God, He is there in the midst of us?

Does God manifest His presence and power in all of these outward expressions? Yes?

Then perhaps God has given us another revelation. You don't have to do any of those things for your salvation. You don't have to anoint with oil or lay hands on the sick or tithe or sing praises to God. The Bible, however, says,

> But be doers of the word, and not hearers only, deceiving yourselves....
> But he...continues in it, and is not a forgetful hearer but a doer of the
> work, this one will be blessed in what he does.   (James 1:22, 25)

Under His Wings

Once, just before Christmas, my wife, Tiz, got very sick. As she was laid up for weeks, I'd go to her every day at around 5:00 a.m. to anoint her with oil and pray for healing, but nothing was happening. Each morning, I prayed to God wearing my tallit, but on this particular morning, God spoke me, saying, "Go into her room now and touch her with the hem of the garment, because Jesus brings healing in His wings." That's what He said. I'm not exaggerating one bit. So, I snuck into the room in the dark where Tiz was deep under the blankets. I touched her with the tassels of the tallit, and she suddenly sat up and threw her arms around me. Like the woman in the marketplace, her healing miracle began that very second.

Was there something magical in this? Not at all. It was certainly nothing of my doing. I don't have enough power in my hands to blow the fuzz off a peach! But my Bible says, *"Lay hands on the sick and they will recover"* (Mark 16:18). Cast out demons and release the power of God.

A Grandmother's Desperation

A couple of months after the Lord miraculously healed Tiz, a lady came up to us after church one Sunday morning. She told us that she had come to church so we could pray for her. She said she was Baptist and a loyal member of her church for years. She had a grandson whom she loved very much. During the prior week, he had been taken to the hospital, where they had discovered several brain aneurysms.

She went to her pastor for prayer. The pastor had heard of the miracles God was doing at New Beginnings, and of Tiz's healing and my teaching on the tallit. After he prayed for her, this pastor suggested that she come and see us.

That morning, I gave her a brief teaching on the woman touching the hem of Jesus' garment. The woman told us that she was going to the hospital to visit her grandson as soon as she left the church. As we prayed for her that morning, I wore my tallit and claimed the healing power of God to come alive for her grandson. On her way out, she stopped by our bookstore and bought one of our tallits.

When she walked into the hospital room, it was filled with many concerned relatives. The woman told them that this was not the way she usually prayed, but she felt the need to obey the Lord in this. She explained to them that, like the woman with the issue of blood, their family had tried everything. She quickly explained what I had told her about the tallit and then laid it on her grandson and prayed for God's promise of healing.

A few hours later, they took more tests on the boy. Not long afterward, the doctor came back into the room with great news: the test showed no more bleeding. By His stripes, her grandson was healed. To God be all the glory.

There are plenty of people who do not believe in laying hands on the sick. To them, all those miracles are just stories in the Bible. To them, we are rolling the dice and hoping that something good will happen. My Bible, however, says that when Jesus comes, there will be healing in His wings. The woman wondered, *If I could touch the hem...if I could touch the wing.* Why? She knew that Jesus did not come as a Protestant or a Gentile but as a Jewish Messiah with healing in His wings.

Wrapped in the Promise

There is an amazing ending to the story of Jesus healing the woman, but it begins with the reason Jesus was rushing through that marketplace to begin with.

There came a man named Jairus, and he was a ruler of the synagogue. And he fell down at Jesus' feet and begged Him to come to his house, for he had an only daughter about twelve years of age, and she was dying. But as He went, the multitudes thronged Him. (Luke 8:41–42)

On most days, the ruler of the synagogue also would have worn the tallit, but in this case, he didn't, because it was customary for a man with a sick child, especially a rabbi, to wrap the child in the tallit—literally to wrap her in the promises of God. So, here was Jairus, in what I can only imagine was a crazed frenzy, rushing Jesus through the marketplace to get to his dying daughter, when this long-suffering woman stopped them. If it had been me, I'm sure I would have urged Jesus not to touch the unclean street woman. She could wait. My daughter was dying. While Jesus was still speaking to the woman, however, someone from Jairus' house arrived with horrible news: "*Your daughter is dead. Do not trouble the Teacher*" (verse 49). Jesus, however, didn't just stop to heal the woman; He also stopped to release greater faith into this father. The father, head of the local synagogue, had already wrapped his child in the promises of God. Now, that same God was showing him that Jesus really did have healing in His wings. Jesus, understanding the man's anguish, said, *"Do not be afraid; only believe, and she will be made well"* (Luke 8:50).

When Jesus arrived at Jairus' house, where the weeping and mourning had begun, He announced, *"Do not weep; she is not dead, but sleeping"* (verse 52). The mourners mocked Jesus for such a foolish statement.

> *But He put them all outside, took her by the hand and called, saying, "Little girl, arise." Then her spirit returned, and she arose immediately. And He commanded that she be given something to eat. And her parents were astonished.* (verses 54–56)

Here was the little girl, wrapped in the tallit—wrapped in the promises of God—and Jesus woke her as if she had only been napping.

Wrapping Yourself in God's Promises

The Psalms contain a prophecy about wearing the prayer shawl:

> *He who dwells in the secret place of the Most High shall abide under the shadow of the Almighty....He shall cover you with His feathers, and under His wings you shall take refuge; His truth shall be your shield and buckler.* (Psalm 91:1, 4)

> **When Jesus said, "Follow Me," He meant, "Imitate Me; walk the way I walk."**

When Jesus said, "Follow Me," He meant "Imitate Me; walk the way I walk; talk the way I talk; eat the way I eat." When we wear prayer shawls, we dwell in the secret place of the Most High God, and in His shadow—under His wings—we will find refuge, healing, deliverance, and prosperity.

When Jewish men put on the tallit, they pray, "How precious is Your kindness, O God. Mankind is in the shelter of Your wings." Of course, we know that God is not a bird with feathers, and that this is not just an analogy—it is prophetic. Jews understood the teachings of Moses. *"Tell them to make tassels on the corners of their garments throughout their generations, and to put a blue thread in the tassels of the corners"* (Numbers 15:38).

I'm not telling you to act weirdly or strangely. I'm not telling you to do anything to be seen by man. Whenever we do things merely to be seen by men, we're already receiving our rewards. I'm just asking: Why not try something that is found in Scripture? Why not get a tallit and wrap yourself in the promises of God as you enter into prayer and worship? You can find them at any synagogue or Jewish supply store, or you can find them on the Internet. They are not very expensive.

I know what you are thinking: *This sort of thing happened only during Jesus' day.* Let me tell you, we have seen miraculous healings that were just as amazing as the one in this story.

Before our services at New Beginnings, I wrap myself in the tallit and pray for my congregation as they enter the building. "That little girl's cancer is gone, in the name of Jesus. Their house is already bought, in the name of Jesus. Those teenagers are not going to be caught up in drugs, in the name of Jesus." As I do this, I am covering my mind with the promises of God. I've experienced a completely new anointing.

One Sunday, the Spirit of God gave me the clear vision that someone at New Beginnings had just found out that he had spots on his liver. During the service, I shared this vision, closed my eyes, and prayed that God would heal whoever it was who had the spots on his liver. When I opened my eyes, there was a lady standing on the platform. Tiz had seen her crying as I gave this word and called her to the platform, where we claimed that prophecy of healing. I could tell you the story, but nobody tells it better than she does.

Healing in His Wings

Last Sunday, New Beginnings prayed for my brother, Steve. Because of those prayers, we were told there are no longer any cancer spots on his liver, and, therefore, no need for a transplant. God is awesome!

Our Lord has done so much in my life these past five months. I want to share it all with you. Several months ago, I was told that

I had a brain aneurysm that could be fixed only through surgery. After prayerful consideration, I said, "I may have one today, but by my Lord's stripes, I am healed." With total peace in my soul, I refused the surgery. A month later, however, I had a stroke that paralyzed the right side of my body.

After the stroke, I was told again that I needed brain surgery and physical therapy in order to recover. Still, in my soul, I refused to believe it. I said, "I'm not moved by what you see because Jesus bore my stroke and aneurysm, and by His stripes, I am healed and made whole."

The next day, the doctor came into my hospital room with a look on her face that I will never forget. She simply said, "The aneurysm is gone." I told her, "So is the numbness in my body." Thanks be to God, I was able to walk out of the hospital that day, healed and made whole.

Amazingly, that is not the end of the miracle. While I was in the hospital, the Lord gave me a Jewish nurse who was with me from the emergency room to my regular room. She overheard me ask my mother to bring me my Bible and tallit. She also heard me quote Isaiah 53 to my doctors: *"He was wounded for our transgressions, He was bruised for our iniquities; the chastisement for our peace was upon Him, and by His stripes we are healed"* (verse 5). She heard me pray using the words "Our Father."

Finally, when we were alone, she asked, "How does a Gentile know Jewish words and how to use the prayer shawl?" That was the opportunity I needed to tell her all about our church and Pastor Larry and his teachings on the Jewish roots of our faith in a Jewish Jesus. She received it all and was there to witness my miracle healing by Jesus, who is the Son of God.

You would think that would be enough, but I'm not done yet. I had a prodigal son whom I had not seen or heard from in years. Three weeks ago, my son suddenly contacted me and announced that he was coming home for a visit. It was extra-meaningful because my birthday was that week. I feel that all of this is the double blessing God has released into my life as I have been obedient to Him. God restored my son and gave me the greatest birthday gift ever!

Once again, I am so grateful to Pastors Larry and Tiz and all that they do. We truly are God's Word wrapped up in flesh. Please keep telling the others what God, Jesus, and the Holy Spirit can do through us and to us.

—Deborah Meeker

You might say, "But Pastor Larry, it is just a physical shawl, a piece of cloth. It has no spiritual powers." And I completely agree with you. But once again, I ask, why do we kneel? Why do we bow our heads? Why do we raise our hands? Those, too, are just physical actions. We do them because physical actions can help connect our minds and consciences with the spiritual. We do them because they put us in the correct mind-set to talk with God. The tallit is no different. It's not a magic cloak. It's a physical reminder of a spiritual truth. You can wrap yourself in it and say, "Father, I claim every one of Your promises through the blood of Jesus. I cover myself in them. I wrap myself in Your healing wings."

The bleeding woman had tried everything. She said, "I'm broke, I'm dying, and I'm unclean, but something about this Man tells me that He is the Messiah with healing in His wings." Then, as she saw the rabbi in the tallit passing by, she reached out and grabbed on to God's promise.

How many of you have tried everything to prosper? How many have tried everything to get delivered from drugs or alcohol addictions? How many have tried everything to heal your families? How many are striving to save and reach your kids? How many of you just need to reach out and grab God's promises?

The Bible says that there will come a day in the end times when the Gentiles, who are hungry for the things of God, will open their eyes to the mysteries of the kingdom. (See Romans 11:25.) They will say, "You know what? We have inherited some lies and the tradition of men along the way, but we are getting rid of all that, and we are getting back to the Word of God. We are going to walk as Jesus walked." In that day, the Bible will no longer be brushed aside as a collection of stories, but it will be cherished as the promise of a living God. When Jesus returns, we are not going home with a moan but with a mighty shout.

As a pastor and a shepherd, as I lay hands on people, my desire is to see God heal them. When I lay hands on people, I want to see them delivered and set free—every one of them.

Keep me as the apple of Your eye; hide me under the shadow of Your wings.   (Psalm 17:8)

I am convinced that the tallit is not a gimmick. It is a taste of what is to come. There are more miraculous blessings found in keeping *Shabbat* and by sharing in the high holy feasts. Let us press on and go deeper into the mysteries and the miracles of *The Torah Blessing*.

6

The Sabbath: Our Appointed Time

I often tell people, "If I could teach you only three things, they would be: first, receive Jesus Christ as your Lord and Savior; second, love Israel—not just the land, but also the people; and third, learn about the miracle God has for you when you *remember* and *keep* the Sabbath." Before we launch into this, let's remember that God's law—His Torah—is not legalism but a process of serving and understanding our heavenly Father. There is miracle power in the appointed day that the Lord calls *Sabbath*—or, in Hebrew, *Shabbat*.

In traditional Judaism, the Sabbath begins on Friday evening and ends at sundown on Saturday. Contrary to popular belief, however, the Sabbath is not meant to designate the day you go to church. No matter when it is, the important thing to keep in mind is that whenever God's people come together to praise and worship Him, the Lord is there. *"Where two or three are gathered together in My name, I am there in the midst of them"* (Matthew 18:20). Here in Dallas, our New Beginnings church meets on Sundays, the same as most other churches in the U.S. We haven't changed the day we meet at the church because we still have the Great Commission to reach the world with the gospel of Jesus Christ—and, for us, Sundays do that best.

New Beginnings also meets on Friday night, however, for our Shabbat service. We do this not out of legalism or empty ritual but for the sake of revelation. In doing so, we have seen a multiplication of the miracle power of God, not only in our personal family, but also in the lives of the family of God. I can't tell you how many times people say to us, "As soon as I started keeping Shabbat, I received a miracle." Bodies have been healed, finances have been released, debts have been canceled, and homes have been restored. I fully believe that miracles like these are waiting for you and that this is the missing element of the Christian walk that you have been waiting for. This is the breakthrough that can connect you to the power of God and to the power that lies in the blood of Jesus.

An Appointed Time

God is God seven days a week. This is something every believer knows. He is Lord Monday through Sunday. "*For I am the* LORD, *I do not change*" (Malachi 3:6). Whenever we need Him, He is *always* there. "*Come to Me, all you who labor and are heavy laden, and I will give you rest*" (Matthew 11:28). The Lord has told us that we can come to Him at anytime, any day of the week, with our needs and concerns.

Even though there is never a time when we cannot get to God, there are special times—appointed times—that the Lord Himself has assigned to meet with us. When dealing with his servants and prophets in Scripture, God often referred to such specific divine appointments:

> *Is anything too hard for the* LORD? *At the appointed time I will return to you, according to the time of life, and Sarah shall have a son.*
> (Genesis 18:14)

> *Then the* LORD *appointed a set time, saying, "Tomorrow the* LORD *will do this thing in the land."* (Exodus 9:5)

> *Is there not an appointed time to man upon earth?* (Job 7:1 KJV)

Appoint means "to fix or set officially, name officially, to arrange for a meeting." God is always there for us to come to Him, but He has set aside a specific time, a fixed and holy time, and it is called the *Sabbath*.

The Ten Commandments that God gave to Moses contain warnings against certain behaviors that can harm our relationship with Him: murder, stealing, adultery, idolatry, etc. They also, however, provide two positive steps that bring us closer to Him: honoring our parents and keeping the Sabbath. God taught His people that doing these things would bring blessings on them and their families, both spiritually and physically. But where did this concept of a Sabbath come from? To understand this, we must go back to the beginning.

God created the heavens and the earth; then, He created light, the sun, and the moon. Then, he created dry land and the oceans with all their living creatures. God created everything we would need to live on this earth.

> *Then God said, "Let the earth bring forth the living creature according to its kind: cattle and creeping thing and beast of the earth, each according to its kind"; and it was so. And God made the beast of the earth according to its kind, cattle according to its kind, and everything that creeps on the earth according to its kind. And God saw that it was good.* (Genesis 1:24–25)

The earth was good. The sea was good. The fruit, the cattle—all of it was good! Why was it good? When you think about it, God had no need for grass or cattle, the sun or the moon. He called everything He created "good" because He knew that it would all be good for *us*.

It was the morning of the sixth day—what we would call Friday. On that day, God gave the world two more good things.

> *Then God said, "Let Us make man in Our image, according to Our likeness; let them have dominion over the fish of the sea, over the birds of the air, and over the cattle, over all the earth and over every creeping thing that creeps on the earth."* (verse 26)

On Friday, the last thing He created was us. On Friday night, God looked over his creation and declared it finished.

> *God saw everything that He had made, and indeed it was very good. So the evening and the morning were the sixth day. Thus the heavens and the earth, and all the host of them, were **finished**. And on the seventh day God **ended His work** which He had done, and He rested on the seventh day from all His work which He had done.* (Genesis 1:31–2:2, emphasis added)

Here's my question: If God *"finished"* everything on the sixth day, what was the work He *"ended"* on the seventh day?

Our Menuhah

Let's begin with the word *rest*. To our Western minds, this means taking the day off. *I've worked six days speaking the universe into being. Now, I'm bushed. I'm exhausted. I need a rest, a break!* Do you really think this is what God was saying? Seems kind of ridiculous, doesn't it? God is all-powerful. He is not a flesh-and-blood man with physical limitations who would be worn out by the end of the day.

In Hebrew, the word *rest* is *menuhah*, meaning "peace, harmony, happiness, no strife." In six days, your heavenly Father created everything that is *"good"* to be a blessing to you. Then, on the evening of the sixth day, the last thing He created was *you!* But His work wasn't complete. It may have been *finished*, but it was not *complete*. In six days, God had created everything man needed to be blessed. On the seventh day, God ended His work by creating the blessing—the menuhah—of peace, joy, happiness, prosperity, and health.

> **Every day we have is a blessed day of God, but the Sabbath is a sanctified day.**

Then God blessed the seventh day and sanctified it, because in it He rested from all His work which God had created and made. (Genesis 2:3)

The Lord blessed and *"sanctified"*—set aside—a day. Every day we have is a blessed day of God, but the Sabbath is a sanctified day—a special day, set aside for you and me. It is a standing, personal appointment with the supernatural promise of God.

Who Is Serving Whom?

I am well aware that most Christians equate the keeping of the Sabbath with religious legalism. This is mostly due to passages of Scripture like this:

Now it happened that [Jesus] went through the grainfields on the Sabbath; and as they went His disciples began to pluck the heads of grain. And the Pharisees said to Him, "Look, why do they do what is not lawful on the Sabbath?" (Mark 2:23–24)

Even in Jesus' day, people tried to take the Torah, the pathway for the people of God to become His lights to the world, and turn it into meaningless legalism. Remember how Jesus responded?

And He said to them, "The Sabbath was made for man, and not man for the Sabbath. Therefore the Son of Man is also Lord of the Sabbath." (Mark 2:27–28)

What powerful Scriptures! The Sabbath—a day of peace, power, and miracles—was given by God to *serve* man; man was never intended to serve the Sabbath. The Sabbath was not a hoop for man to jump through in order to please his master. God's Word urges us to keep the Sabbath because *it* is to serve *us*; it is an appointment with our Creator, made available through the sacrifice of Jesus Christ. That is why Jesus made His claim to be *"Lord of the Sabbath."* He is the one who connects every man, woman, and child to this Sabbath rest, the menuhah.

Laboring for Our Rest

As Christians, we have been taught that God's Word *"is living and powerful, and sharper than any two-edged sword, piercing even to the division of soul and spirit, and of joints and marrow, and is a discerner of the thoughts and intents of the heart"* (Hebrews 4:12). We have often heard and read these words penned by the writer of Hebrews. But what was the author specifically getting at? To understand this, we must look at the verses preceding it:

For He has spoken in a certain place of the seventh day in this way: "And God rested on the seventh day from all His works"; and again in this place: "They shall not enter My rest." Since therefore it remains that some must enter it, and those to whom it was first preached did not enter because of disobedience, again He designates a certain day, saying in David, "Today," after such a long time, as it has been said: "Today, if you will hear His voice, do not harden your hearts." For if Joshua had given them rest, then He would not afterward have spoken of another day. There remains therefore a rest for the people of God.

For he who has entered His rest has himself also ceased from his works as God did from His. Let us therefore be diligent to enter that rest, lest anyone fall according to the same example of disobedience. For the word of God is living and powerful, and sharper than any two-edged sword, piercing even to the division of soul and spirit, and of joints and marrow, and is a discerner of the thoughts and intents of the heart.

(Hebrews 4:4–12)

> **When we enter His rest, the Word of God is able to penetrate our spirits and souls to work its way into our hearts.**

When we enter His rest, the Word of God is able to penetrate our spirits and souls to work its way into our hearts. We who believe in Jesus Christ, who have been grafted into Israel, have a right to enter into this rest—the menuhah. This rest was first shown to some who didn't receive it because they had hardened their hearts. The writer warned his readers, "*do not harden your hearts.*" In verse 9, he assured us, "*There remains therefore a rest for the people of God.*"

Look at verse 11: "*Let us therefore be diligent to enter that rest, lest anyone fall according to the same example of disobedience.*" In the King James Version, the word *diligent* is translated as "*labor.*" He seems to be saying, "Let us *make an effort* to enter into this rest." Some have missed this rest because of hardened hearts. Others have missed it because of a lack of understanding or a fear of legalism. We are saved by grace, not by the law, but we need to add knowledge to our faith so that we don't miss this rest, as well. According to Hebrews, this may take some *effort* on our part.

Remembering and Keeping the Sabbath

There are two words most often associated with the Sabbath: *remember* and *keep*.

__Remember__ the Sabbath day, to __keep__ it holy. Six days you shall labor and do all your work, but the seventh day is the Sabbath of the LORD your God. In it you shall do no work: you, nor your son, nor your

daughter, nor your male servant, nor your female servant, nor your
cattle, nor your stranger who is within your gates. For in six days the
LORD made the heavens and the earth, the sea, and all that is in them,
and rested the seventh day. Therefore the LORD blessed the Sabbath
day and hallowed it.   (Exodus 20:8–11, emphasis added)

Remembering

In Hebrew, *remember* is the word *zakar*. In *Strong's Hebrew Dictionary*, it means "to mark…to remember; by implication, to mention; also to be male." In Hebrew culture, the firstborn male child was someone special, different from any other. *"All the firstborn of man among your sons you shall redeem"* (Exodus 13:13). In the same way, we are told by God to *"remember the Sabbath."* Of all the days of the week, the Sabbath is special, different from any other.

Keeping

Then the next phrase in Exodus 20:8 is *"keep it holy."* It is not enough just to remember it, but we need to keep it, also. We need to set it aside as something holy. This goes with the writer of Hebrews urging for us to make an effort not to miss this miraculous time with God. The opposite of *keeping* something would be *losing* it. God seems to be warning us that the Sabbath is something we need to keep, or continue, lest we start to forget and let it fade away until it is lost for good.

I firmly believe that we should never take one verse of Scripture and make a doctrine or a teaching out of it. That said, let's look at just a few more Scriptures that teach about the Sabbath as the day God has given to all of us.

Then he said to them, "This is what the LORD has said: 'Tomorrow is
a Sabbath rest, a holy Sabbath to the LORD.'"   (Exodus 16:23)

Therefore the children of Israel shall keep the Sabbath, to observe the
Sabbath throughout their generations as a perpetual covenant.
(Exodus 31:16)

Observe the Sabbath day, to keep it holy, as the LORD your God com-
manded you....And remember that you were a slave in the land of
Egypt, and the LORD your God brought you out from there by a mighty
hand and by an outstretched arm; therefore the LORD your God com-
manded you to keep the Sabbath day.   (Deuteronomy 5:12, 15)

> **As Christians, we forget that we were once slaves to sin and in need of deliverance.**

As we take time in our busy lives to stop for the Sabbath, we must keep in mind that we are *in this world,* but we are not *of this world.* Like Israel when they exited Egypt, we are delivered from enslavement to the world through Jesus Christ. Something else we are prone to forgetting is that we were once slaves. I'm sure that after a few generations in the Promised Land, Israel's history of slavery would have begun to fade away, were it not for their Sabbath and Passover remembrances. Likewise, as Christians, we sometimes forget that we were once slaves to sin and in need of deliverance. The Sabbath is a great time to reflect on that and appreciate the fact that *"God brought you out from there by a mighty hand and by an outstretched arm."*

Sabbath Begins at Sundown

Many Christians' only experience seeing a biblical Sabbath celebrated is in the movie *Fiddler on the Roof.* In one scene, the family is scurrying around on the day before the Sabbath. The main character in the movie is Tevye, the man who delivers milk and cheese to a small Russian town. Golde, his wife, grows angry because Tevye still has deliveries to make, and it is almost sundown, the beginning of the Sabbath and time for their Shabbat family dinner. "Hurry," she says, "you'll be late!"

Why does God insist that the Sabbath begin at sundown? Is He being legalistic? I think it is because He knows us better than we know ourselves. He knows of our tendency to fill our lives with seemingly critical obligations and requirements. Left to our own devices, we tend to keep ourselves so hurried and busy that we forget Him, the One from whom our blessings come. Because God knows this about us, He gave us a commandment to set aside one day, beginning at a specific time, for an appointment with Him. He even gave the appointment a name: the Sabbath. He assigned a specific day of each week, the seventh day, so we wouldn't be confused and miss it. By seeking Him on this day, we receive all the peace, blessing, joy, prosperity, and happiness that God has promised us. God knows we are busy. He knows we have work to do. He also knows, however, that we will never achieve all that is before us if we charge ahead without His blessing and provision. Does that sound like bondage or legalism? To me, it sounds like good news and freedom.

Now, let us address "the elephant in the room." Throughout history, the Jewish Sabbath has begun at sundown Friday and has gone until sundown on Saturday. After Christ's resurrection, the Christian Sabbath eventually landed on the morning of the first day of the week. How did that happen? Have you ever wondered when and why the Christian day of worship changed from Saturday to Sunday?

Has the Sabbath Day Changed?

God's Word tells us that God blessed the seventh day and made it holy—an appointed day.

> *The LORD spoke to Moses, saying, "Speak also to the children of Israel, saying: 'Surely My Sabbaths you shall keep, for it is a sign between Me and you throughout your generations, that you may know that I am the LORD who sanctifies you. You shall keep the Sabbath, therefore, for it is holy to you. Everyone who profanes it shall surely be put to death; for whoever does any work on it, that person shall be cut off from among his people."* (Exodus 31:12–14)

Obviously, if we don't keep the Sabbath, God is not going to kill us. That would be ridiculous. Let's examine, therefore, the physical and spiritual sides of what God was saying. Could it be that when we fail to physically keep and remember the Sabbath, the spiritual blessings and miracles that God has for us will die? Perhaps we have not seen and experienced all the Lord has for us because we have lost this miraculous, appointed time of God's rest. Could it be that we have missed out on healing and blessings for our finances and families?

How, then, did the church change one of the Ten Commandments from Saturday to Sunday? Did God change it, or did man?

The Big Switch

*Now on the first **day** of the week, when the disciples came together to break bread, Paul, ready to depart the next day, spoke to them and continued his message until midnight.* (Acts 20:7, emphasis added)

This is the passage of Scripture most often used to make the case that Paul and the early church changed the Sabbath from Saturday, the seventh day of the week, to Sunday, the first day of the week.

Look up this same passage in your Bible. Do you see something different about the printing of the word *day*? If you're reading from the King James translation or the *New King James Version* of the Bible, it should be the only italicized word in the sentence. Do you know why some words in Scripture are in italics? This denotes instances where words were added for clarity—words that were not in the original text but were added centuries later, usually to make a point or to clarify the translated meaning of the passage.

The original text reads, "*On motza' el-shabbat, when the disciples came together to break bread….*" Modern translations have traditionally replaced *motza' el-shabbat* with the word *day* when its actual meaning is "at the end of the Sabbath." (See *The Complete Jewish Bible* by David Stern.)

In the Gregorian calendar, the last day of the calendar week is Saturday, the seventh day. Sunday morning then begins the first day. Biblically, however, days begin and end at sundown. Therefore, the first day of the week begins not Sunday morning but on Saturday evening, specifically after the first three visible stars. By eliminating the word *day* from Acts 20:7, the time *"the disciples came together to break bread"* was actually Saturday evening, the end of the Sabbath, and not Sunday morning. Let's look at reasons why.

First, it is a custom to start the Sabbath at sunset on Friday evening when you break bread and share a Sabbath meal with your friends and family. It is a meaningful time of fun and fellowship. The Sabbath officially ends on Saturday evening when three stars can be seen in the sky. This is the beginning of the next week. There is a traditional service to end the Sabbath call *havdalah*, where candles are lit and blessings are spoken. Although this is the technical end of the Sabbath, its spirit continues into the night with a meal and the breaking of bread.

Second, Acts 20:7 says that Paul spoke to them until midnight, then *"talked a long while, even till daybreak"* (verse 11). Doesn't that make more sense than Paul preaching from Sunday morning all the way until midnight? Even for me, eighteen hours of preaching would be a long time. This verse, therefore, actually supports Saturday as being the Sabbath recognized by Paul and the other apostles.

Does it really matter, though? What if the first day of the week was Monday or Tuesday? Most of us have probably been to church at one time or another on every day of the week, usually going out to fellowship and "break bread" afterward. It still doesn't change God's Word. The writer of the book of Hebrews said that there is a special day—the seventh day. *"Let us therefore be diligent to enter that rest"* (Hebrews 4:11). If Moses taught the Sabbath, and Isaiah taught it, and Paul taught it, and Jesus taught it, then how did it come to be changed from Saturday to Sunday?

Politics and Anti-Semitism

Eventually, as the early church grew and spread across the world, the Gentile believers in Jesus Christ outpaced the Jewish believers. As in everything in this world, when man gets involved, so does human error, politics, and greed. Church leaders, for many reasons, began to separate themselves and the church from the Hebrew roots of the Scriptures, from anything Jewish, and from Israel itself. Eventually, the church turned from Israel to Rome in mind, spirit, and doctrine. This parting of the ways between Christians and Jews took place gradually over a period of two or three centuries.

> As in everything in this world, when man gets involved, so does human error, politics, and greed.

Although there is no evidence in Scripture or historical Christian documents that the disciples celebrated what is now called "Easter," it was an established tradition in the church by the beginning of the second century. Such a celebration of the resurrection of Jesus, the Lamb of God, certainly was linked on the calendar with the Jewish celebration of Passover and the Jews' observance of the Sabbath—taking place on Saturday.

In A.D. 135, the Roman emperor Hadrian outlawed keeping the Sabbath altogether. Thus, it was a man, not God, who declared it illegal to keep the Sabbath on Saturday—as had been the custom according to the Word of God and the practice of Jesus and His followers.

Three hundred years after the resurrection of Jesus, a man named Flavius Valerius Aurelius Constantinus—better known as Constantine the Great—became emperor of Rome. He became known as the first "Christian" emperor. Constantine felt that he was responsible to God for the spiritual health of the people. He made it the law of Rome that God would be "properly worshipped" in his empire. Of course, what was deemed "proper" was determined by his completely Gentile and politically motivated church. In A.D. 325, Constantine arranged what would be called the Council of Nicea to determine what was approved church doctrine and what was heresy. Among their many decrees was the decision to change the custom of Christians celebrating Passover on the fourteenth day of the Hebrew month of Nisan. This was a date set in the Torah:

> So this day shall be to you a memorial; and you shall keep it as a feast to the LORD throughout your generations. You shall keep it as a feast by an everlasting ordinance. (Exodus 12:14)

> On the fourteenth day of the first month at twilight is the LORD's Passover. (Leviticus 23:5)

The Word of God says this was a fixed date—"an everlasting ordinance." Three hundred years after the death of Christ, however, Constantine and the Council of Nicea prohibited Christians from remembering and celebrating Jesus on Saturday and moved the Sabbath to Sunday. This was the beginning of a systematic separation of Christianity from its Jewish roots. Emperor Constantine made this declaration:

> Sunday will now be a day of rest for the whole Roman Empire, the venerable Day of the Sun. Let magistrates and people residing in cities rest and let all workshops be closed. In the country, however,

persons engaged in agriculture may freely and lawfully continue their pursuits because it often happens that another day is not suitable for grain-sowing or for vine-planting; lest by neglecting the proper moment for such operations the bounty of Heaven should be lost.[4]

There were two reasons for this. First, the Christian church had suffered great persecution from some Jews who had rejected Christ. Relations between the two groups had grown quite hostile at that time. Second, as Rome was stepping up its persecution of Jews, it seemed an appropriate time to separate Christianity from Judaism as much as possible.

In A.D. 364, the Council of Laodicea declared that all Christian observance was to be conducted on Sunday, not Saturday. By order of the council, Sunday was the new Sabbath.

Christians shall not Judaize and be idle on Saturday, the Sabbath, but shall work on that day; but the Lord's day [Sunday] they shall especially honor, and, as being Christians, shall, if possible, do no work on that day. If, however, they are found Judaizing, they shall be shut out from Christ.[5]

Not only were Christians being driven from their Jewish roots—and the revelation of God's Word, the Torah—but they were also being told not to "Judaize." In other words, don't be like the Jews. Don't be like Jews such as Abraham, Moses, Daniel, Ezekiel, or Isaiah. Don't be like Jews such as Peter, Paul, or even Jesus. Paul declared that non-Jewish believers were *"once Gentiles…having no hope and without God in the world"* (Ephesians 2:11–12). He claimed that now they were *"no longer strangers and foreigners, but fellow citizens with the saints and members of the household of God, having been built on the foundation of the apostles and prophets, Jesus Christ Himself being the chief cornerstone"* (verses 19–20). Gentile believers were once without a family or covenant with God, but, thanks to the blood of Jesus, they had been *"grafted in"* (Romans 11:17). Now, the church was saying, "Christians shall not Judaize." Unfortunately, this was only the beginning.

---

[4] *Codex Justinianus*, lib. 12:3.
[5] Canon 29, Council of Laodicea.

Jewish Persecution

Have you ever wondered why the devil has worked for thousands of years to destroy Israel and the Jewish people? Beginning in the time of Jesus, the Roman Empire murdered thousands of Jews, including Jesus, eventually sacking Jerusalem itself. The early church fathers, including Eusebius, Cyril, Chrysostom, Augustine, Origen, Justin, and Jerome, all taught against the Jews, calling them such hateful terms as "Christ killers." John Chrysostom (A.D. 345–407), considered the greatest preacher of the Eastern Orthodox Church and called the "Bishop with the Golden Mouth," once claimed,

> The Jews are the most worthless of all men. They are lecherous, greedy, and rapacious. They are perfidious murders of Christ. They worship the devil; their religion is a sickness. The Jews are the odious assassins of Christ and for killing God there is no explanation possible, no indulgence or pardon. Christians may never cease vengeance and the Jews must live in servitude forever. God always hated the Jews. It is incumbent upon all Christians to hate the Jew.[6]

This type of anti-Semitism has existed throughout the world over the last seventeen hundred years. During the Crusades, the rallying cry for the Christian soldiers was, "Kill a Jew and save your soul!" On July 15, 1099, Jerusalem was captured by the Crusaders. Most of the Jewish population, an estimated twenty to thirty thousand, was slaughtered.

During the Spanish Inquisitions (established in 1478 and not abolished until 1834), Jews were given a choice: leave Spain and forfeit all land and property to the church, or convert to Catholicism. The total number of Jews affected varies, depending on the source, but the true number is probably around eighty thousand, out of which one-half left; the other half, out of a need for survival, converted. These *conversos* were the principal aim of the church and the Inquisition of 1483. Spanish citizens were to turn in *maranos*, as they were called, meaning "damned," "accursed," or "hogs." They were easy to spot. One had only to climb to the rooftops on a Saturday. No smoke would be rising from Jewish homes, in spite of the cold weather, for they were not allowed to build fires on the Sabbath.

---

[6] John Chrysostom homily, "Orations against the Jews."

Martin Luther, the German father of the Protestant Reformation, was well-known for his anti-Semitic views. In 1543, he wrote a treatise, "On the Jews and Their Lies," in which he claimed that the Jews were a "base, whoring people, that is, no people of God, and their boast of lineage, circumcision, and law must be accounted as filth."[7] He said they were full of the "devil's feces...which they wallow in like swine."[8] Luther urged that their synagogues and schools be set on fire, prayer books be destroyed, rabbis be forbidden to preach, and property and money be confiscated. He also suggested that they be forced into slave camps or permanently expelled. In the end, he said, "we are at fault in not slaying them."[9]

It was views like these that influenced generations of German thinking, which eventually helped to fuel Adolf Hitler and the Nazis' "Final Solution," an attempt to completely exterminate the entire Jewish race. For what problem could such barbaric schemes be considered a "solution"?

The devil's "problem" is true Christian faith. Why has he tried for so many centuries to wipe out the Jewish race and destroy Israel? It is simple. The Jews are the keepers of God's Word. They are the branches that come from the Root. If Satan cannot kill the Root, he can certainly attempt to cut off and destroy the branches. Part of this strategy has included separating the grafted branches—Christianity—from the tree of Judaism. Better yet, he gets them to argue, fight, hate, and even kill one another. Once again, *"making the word of God of no effect through your tradition which you have handed down"* (Mark 7:13).

> **If Satan cannot kill the Root, he can certainly attempt to cut off and destroy the branches.**

The Sabbath—A Holy Time

Let me show you another reason why the Sabbath has been such a target for the enemy. If I were to ask you, "What is the most holy thing to

[7] Martin Luther, "On the Jews and Their Lies," cited in Robert Michael, *Holy Hatred: Christianity, Anti-Semitism, and the Holocaust* (New York: Palgrave Macmillan, 2006), 111.
[8] Ibid., 113.
[9] Martin Luther, "On the Jews and Their Lies," cited in Robert Michael, "Luther, Luther Scholars, and the Jews," *Encounter 46*, no. 4 (Autumn 1985), 343–344.

God?" what would your answer be? The Bible? The Torah? Jerusalem, His holy city? Or perhaps Calvary, the place where Jesus Christ, the Lamb of God, died for you and me? All these things are wonderfully holy. But to God, what is the most holy thing? Perhaps the most holy thing to God is not a geographical place but a place in time. Let's return once again to the book of Genesis:

> *And on the seventh day God ended His work which He had done, and He rested on the seventh day from all His work which He had done. Then God blessed the seventh day and sanctified it, because in it He rested from all His work which God had created and made.*
>
> (Genesis 2:2–3)

According to *Webster's New Collegiate Dictionary*, to *sanctify* something is "to set apart to a sacred purpose...purify...to make productive of holiness." When God finished creating the heavens, the earth, and all creatures great and small, there was only one thing that He called holy: the seventh day, the Sabbath. God *"blessed the seventh day and sanctified it."* If creation had been up to me, I most likely would have created some kind of "holy" architecture—perhaps a grand temple or an ornate palace for believers to visit on pilgrimages.

Instead, God gave us a period of time to pause and remember Him each week. There was a time when God's presence dwelt in the tabernacle of Moses and the temple of Solomon. As wonderful as they were, these were places built by the hands of men that could also be destroyed by the hands of men. The "Tabernacle of the Sabbath," however, was made not by man but by God. Man has tried to tear it down, but he cannot. It is a secret place—a holy place. It is the Holy of Holies, which was once forbidden for sinful man to enter, but which is now available to all who believe because Jesus has torn the curtain from top to bottom. God beckons. Go in and meet with Him. The miracle power of God awaits you!

7

What Would Jesus Do?
First, He'd Admit That He's a Jew!

When Jesus called people to be His disciples, it was with one repeated refrain: "*Follow Me.*"

> *When He had called the people to Himself, with His disciples also, He said to them, "Whoever desires to come after Me, let him deny himself, and take up his cross, and follow Me."* (Mark 8:34)

> *So when Jesus heard these things, He said to him, "You still lack one thing. Sell all that you have and distribute to the poor, and you will have treasure in heaven; and come, follow Me."* (Luke 18:22)

> *My sheep hear My voice, and I know them, and they follow Me.* (John 10:27)

> *If anyone serves Me, let him follow Me; and where I am, there My servant will be also. If anyone serves Me, him My Father will honor.* (John 12:26)

We know that Jesus was not telling people simply to walk behind Him. He was urging His followers to imitate His life, to be like Him. As children of God, I think we would all agree that our ultimate goal is to be like Jesus. According to *Strong's Concordance*, part of the root word of *follow* in Greek is the word for *road*. This makes sense if we remember that the Torah, God's law, is not legalism but a path that leads us to God's blessing.

The Faith of Jesus

So He came to Nazareth, where He had been brought up. And as His custom was, He went into the synagogue on the Sabbath day, and stood up to read. (Luke 4:16)

Here we see Jesus, early in His ministry, going into a synagogue on the Sabbath day because it was His custom to do so. Jesus and His family were observant Jews who followed the Torah. From His very birth, Jesus was raised according to all the teachings and requirements of the Torah.

And when eight days were completed for the circumcision of the Child, His name was called JESUS, the name given by the angel before He was conceived in the womb. Now when the days of her purification according to the law of Moses were completed, they brought Him to Jerusalem to present Him to the Lord (as it is written in the law of the Lord, "Every male who opens the womb shall be called holy to the LORD"). (Luke 2:21–23)

A Teacher of the Torah

As Jesus grew up, every year, His parents took Him on the 140-mile trip to Jerusalem for Passover. By the time He was twelve, Jesus had trouble leaving the temple to go home.

His parents went to Jerusalem every year at the Feast of the Passover. And when He was twelve years old, they went up to Jerusalem according to the custom of the feast. When they had finished the days, as they returned, the Boy Jesus lingered behind in Jerusalem. And Joseph and His mother did not know it; but supposing Him to have been in the company, they went a day's journey, and sought Him among their relatives and acquaintances. So when they did not find Him, they returned to Jerusalem, seeking Him. Now so it was that after three days they found Him in the temple, sitting in the midst of the teachers, both listening to them and asking them questions. And all who heard Him were astonished at His understanding and answers. (Luke 2:41–47)

Even at a young age, Jesus had a firm understanding of the Torah, the Word of God. *"And He said to them, 'Why did you seek Me? Did you not know that I must be about My Father's business?'"* (verse 49).

He later referred to the temple as *"My Father's house"* (John 2:16). As He progressed and built His ministry, His disciples, followers, and even the Pharisees called Him "Rabbi"—a teacher of the Torah.

> *In the meantime His disciples urged Him, saying, "Rabbi, eat."*
> (John 4:31)

> *Jesus said to her, "Mary!" She turned and said to Him, "Rabboni!" (which is to say, Teacher).* (John 20:16)

> *There was a man of the Pharisees named Nicodemus, a ruler of the Jews. This man came to Jesus by night and said to Him, "Rabbi, we know that You are a teacher come from God; for no one can do these signs that You do unless God is with him."* (John 3:1–2)

Jesus and the Sabbath

> *Then they went into Capernaum, and immediately on the Sabbath He entered the synagogue and taught.* (Mark 1:21)

Jesus came to Capernaum and immediately went to the synagogue. Why? It was the Sabbath.

> *And when the Sabbath had come, He began to teach in the synagogue. And many hearing Him were astonished, saying, "Where did this Man get these things? And what wisdom is this which is given to Him, that such mighty works are performed by His hands!"* (Mark 6:2)

Jesus and Passover

Much of Jesus' ministry revolved around the celebration of Passover.

> *Now the Passover of the Jews was at hand, and Jesus went up to Jerusalem.* (John 2:13)

Now on the first day of the Feast of the Unleavened Bread the disciples came to Jesus, saying to Him, "Where do You want us to prepare for You to eat the Passover?" And He said, "Go into the city to a certain man, and say to him, 'The Teacher says, "My time is at hand; I will keep the Passover at your house with My disciples."'" So the disciples did as Jesus had directed them; and they prepared the Passover. When evening had come, He sat down with the twelve. (Matthew 26:17–20)

Jesus and the High Holy Days

Jesus kept the fall festivals, such as the Feast of the Tabernacles.

Now the Jews' Feast of Tabernacles was at hand....But when His brothers had gone up, then He also went up to the feast, not openly, but as it were in secret....Now about the middle of the feast Jesus went up into the temple and taught. (John 7:2, 10, 14)

In the winter, Jesus celebrated Hanukkah.

Now it was the Feast of Dedication in Jerusalem, and it was winter. And Jesus walked in the temple, in Solomon's porch. (John 10:22–23)

I realize that this is a lot of Scripture to throw at you, but as we look deeper in the miracle powers of the Sabbath, I want you to recognize the "Torah Road" that Jesus paved and walked for the entire world to follow.

Jesus and Sabbath Miracles

Clearly, Scripture shows us that Jesus was not only an observant Jew, but also that He and His whole family faithfully followed God's Torah. When Jesus began His ministry, however, amazing things began to happen. According to the apostle John, the miracles of Jesus were so numerous that *"if they were written one by one, I suppose that even the world itself could not contain the books that would be written"* (John 21:25). Of all these miracles, however, the writers of the Gospels recorded seven specific miracles that Jesus performed on the Sabbath. Here are the seven miracles listed in their probable chronological order:

1. Healing of a man with an unclean spirit. (See Mark 1:21–31; Luke 4:31–37.)

2. Healing of Peter's mother-in-law. (See Matthew 8:14–15; Mark 1:29–31; Luke 4:38–39.)

3. Healing of a man with a withered hand. (See Matthew 12:9–14; Mark 3:1–6; Luke 6:6–10.)

4. Healing of a paralyzed man at the pools of Bethesda. (See John 5:1–18.)

5. Healing of a woman who had a spirit of infirmity. (See Luke 13:10–17.)

6. Healing of a man with dropsy. (See Luke 14:1–4.)

7. Healing of a man blind from birth. (See John 9:1–16.)

Seven recorded miracles were performed on the seventh day of the week—the Sabbath—the day God set aside and made holy since the very beginning of time. In fact, this was one of the chief reasons that the Pharisees became angry with Jesus and watched Him so closely. To these religious leaders, the Sabbath was reserved for man's traditions, rules, and regulations.

Over and over, however, Jesus performed these miracles to demonstrate that keeping and remembering the Sabbath has nothing to do with legalism. Rather, the Sabbath was (and is) a special time appointed by God for His people to meet with Him, that He might touch every area of their lives and lead them into His rest—*menuhah*—a time of peace, healing, and miracle provision.

> **Keeping and remembering the Sabbath has nothing to do with legalism.**

The Sabbath is made to serve you and bring you God's miracle rest. It is not a test or a religious hoop for you to jump through in order to please Him—or anybody else.

The Sabbath after Jesus

We've seen many examples from Scripture of Jesus keeping the Sabbath. What about His disciples? Did they follow Him concerning the Sabbath, or did their customs change after Jesus died?

Now behold, there was a man named Joseph....This man went to Pilate and asked for the body of Jesus. Then he took it down, wrapped it in linen, and laid it in a tomb that was hewn out of the rock, where no one had ever lain before. That day was the Preparation, and the Sabbath drew near. And the women who had come with Him from Galilee followed after, and they observed the tomb and how His body was laid. Then they returned and prepared spices and fragrant oils. And they rested on the Sabbath according to the commandment.

(Luke 23:50, 52–56)

Now when the Sabbath was past, Mary Magdalene, Mary the mother of James, and Salome bought spices, that they might come and anoint Him. (Mark 16:1)

Here, we see some of Jesus' followers immediately after He died on the cross balancing His burial preparations with their observance of the Sabbath.

Likewise, throughout the book of Acts, Paul and Barnabas kept the Sabbath as they planted churches and preached the good news:

But when they departed from Perga, they came to Antioch in Pisidia, and went into the synagogue on the Sabbath day and sat down. And after the reading of the Law and the Prophets, the rulers of the synagogue sent to them, saying, "Men and brethren, if you have any word of exhortation for the people, say on." (Acts 13:14–15)

And on the Sabbath day we went out of the city to the riverside, where prayer was customarily made; and we sat down and spoke to the women who met there. (Acts 16:13)

Then Paul, as his custom was, went in to them, and for three Sabbaths reasoned with them from the Scriptures. (Acts 17:2)

And he reasoned in the synagogue every Sabbath, and persuaded both Jews and Greeks. (Acts 18:4)

Thus, keeping and remembering the Sabbath did not go out of fashion with the death of Jesus. On the contrary, it seems like it was front and center in the life of the apostles' preaching.

Once again, I'm not suggesting that you find another church that meets on Saturday. I'm simply suggesting that you begin by allowing God to touch your life in a very special way on the Sabbath as Jesus and His followers did.

A Shadow of Things to Come

As I have stated before, the observance of the Sabbath is not legalism, but a gift from God—a day that He Himself blessed.

> *Every good gift and every perfect gift is from above, and comes down from the Father of lights, with whom there is no variation or shadow of turning.* (James 1:17)

Since the Bible is full of the healing miracles that Jesus purposefully performed on the Sabbath, and since we also know from Scripture that, one day, there will be no more sickness, hunger, or tears, could it be that God has provided this one day in His rest—menuhah—as a brief glimpse or taste of what is to come to all of us through Jesus?

> *So let no one judge you in food or in drink, or regarding a festival or a new moon or sabbaths, which are a shadow of things to come, but the substance is of Christ.* (Colossians 2:16–17)

I don't know about you, but I was always taught that Paul was saying, "Don't let anybody tell you what you can't eat, tell you to keep the holy days, or try to 'Judaize' you by keeping the Sabbath." Maybe you were taught something similar. It was made clear that such commandments were not for Christians because we were no longer *"under the curse"* (Galatians 3:10) of the law. What was Paul saying to us in Colossians? To find out, let's go back a few verses:

> *As you have therefore received Christ Jesus the Lord, so **walk in Him**, rooted and built up in Him and established in the faith, as you have*

been taught, abounding in it with thanksgiving. Beware lest anyone cheat you through philosophy and empty deceit, according to the tradition of men, according to the basic principles of the world, and not according to Christ. (Colossians 2:6–8, emphasis added)

"Walk in Him," Paul said. "Follow Him; do what He did; serve God the way He did." How did Jesus walk? One of the ways He walked was by keeping and remembering the Sabbath, and by celebrating Passover and other holy days, as did His disciples. Paul urged his readers not to let *"the tradition of men"*—which would eventually include the Council of Nicea—change the way they walked in Christ. Then, in verses 16 and 17, he said to let no man *"judge you"* because you eat what Jesus ate or because you celebrate Passover and keep the Sabbath the way Jesus did. According to Paul, these things are a *"shadow of things to come"* (verse 17).

> **The Sabbath, this miracle rest that we are given every week, is a shadow of the realities of heaven.**

As I sit at my desk writing these words, the shadow of my hand covers part of the paper. That shadow is of my actual hand, not a copy or fake version of my hand. When you see a shadow coming around the corner, it's an image of the real thing that is coming. The Sabbath, this miracle rest that we are given every week, is a shadow of the realities of heaven.

Rabbi Abraham Heschel was an American rabbi born in Warsaw, Poland, who was considered one of the leading Jewish theologians of the twentieth century. He once wrote, regarding the Sabbath, "The essence of the world to come is Sabbath eternal, and the seventh day in time is an example of eternity…a foretaste of the world to come."[10] The word for *bride* in Hebrew is the word *kallah*. In Jewish literature, the Sabbath is often referred to as "the Sabbath Bride." The picture of a bride is love, devotion, and joy. It's an inward feeling. This feeling is renewed and made fresh every Sabbath.

One of the things I love to do most is taking people to Israel. I always take groups to the Sea of Galilee first. After four or five days, I love to

---

[10] Abraham Heschel, *The Sabbath* (New York: Farrar, Straus and Giroux, 1951), 74.

watch the expressions on people's faces as we start climbing the Judean hills on our approach to Jerusalem. I always time our entry into the holy city of God to coincide with the time when the people there are preparing for Sabbath. It is a supernatural time. The whole city is preparing for the Sabbath Bride. It's tremendous. If you are ever able to experience this, it will change your life.

A saying many Jewish and Christian children are taught, including my own children and grandchildren, goes like this: "Remember, children, the days pass swiftly. The holy Sabbath approaches and knocks upon the door." In the very beginning of God's Word, in Genesis, we were given a blessed, sanctified day in which to find our rest in Him. It is a foretaste of God's miracle power. At the very end of God's Word, in Revelation, Jesus told us,

> *Behold, I stand at the door and knock. If anyone hears My voice and opens the door, I will come in to him and dine with him, and he with Me.* (Revelation 3:20)

It is also said that the Sabbath allows us to touch the hem of the world to come. What a beautiful reminder of the woman with the issue of blood who reached out and touched the hem of the garment worn by Jesus—the Lord of the Sabbath.

> *And Jesus said, "Who touched me?...Somebody touched Me, for I perceived power going out from me."* (Luke 8:45–46)

Maybe you're like this woman who struggled with an illness for twelve years. She had seen many doctors, and nothing had given her relief. Jesus, the Lord of the Sabbath, is walking by. God is ready to release the miracle that the Lord has for you, *right now*. It pleases Him to give His children a foretaste of all the blessings that will one day be ours for all of eternity. This Friday night—the Sabbath—why don't you reach out and touch the hem of Jesus' garment?

You are probably wondering, *How do I so that? Where do I start? What if I do it wrong?* Remember, the Sabbath is not about legalism; it's not about a list of dos and don'ts. It's a special day, an appointed time. It is a time in which the Lord wants to touch all that you've been working and praying for all week. As the sun goes down on Friday evening, just stop and say,

> Lord, right now, I welcome the Sabbath peace (*Shabbat shalom*) into my life, my children, my marriage, my finances, my health, and my future.

You will begin to feel a supernatural peace, and you will begin to experience the miracle power of God. After this small step, I have no doubt that you will want to go deeper and learn more. Ladies, you will want to learn, as wives and mothers, how God uses you to light the Sabbath candles and speak the Sabbath prayer so that the light of God will always shine, no matter how dark it gets outside your homes.

In the next chapter, I will go into the celebration of the Sabbath in detail. In no time, you can be speaking God's blessing over your marriage, prophesying God's plan over your children, welcoming God's joy in your home, and releasing God's double portion into your finances. Join us and experience the miracle of *Shabbat shalom*—or Sabbath peace.

8

A Shabbat for All People

s we approach the Sabbath, I must remind you of something that my rabbi friends tell me: "It is never all or nothing." In other words, if you do one thing wrong, you do not ruin the integrity of the Sabbath. That Sabbath was made for you. It is not your responsibility to perfectly perform some ritual in order to please God. Earlier, I explained that one of the reasons we keep the Sabbath is because it is one of the Ten Commandments in which God said to remember it and keep it. We've seen that Jesus and His disciples kept the Sabbath, and we've learned how the writer of Hebrews instructed us to be diligent to enter into this Sabbath rest because some miss it. Unfortunately, a lot of us have missed it because nobody has taught us. As I said in the beginning, it is not the truth that will make us free, but the truth we know and understand that will make us free.

The Sabbath table is prepared for dinner with a few specific items for our celebration, each of which I will explain: a tzedakah box, two candles, a goblet or glass filled to the brim with wine or grape juice, the challah bread, and a salt shaker.

Preparations

Let me say at this point that Shabbat is not a solemn church service. It is a celebration of God's blessings. Once Shabbat begins, you cannot be sad or stern. This is a time to be full of life. Don't worry, therefore, about your kids running around or laughing and playing. You are releasing the

Sabbath joy and blessing on your family. This is a time your family should treasure and look forward to, not a time they dread.

Here are the items you should set on your table before the sun sets:

+ a small box or other receptacle for coins
+ two candlesticks
+ a clear cup or goblet filled to the brim with red wine or grape juice
+ a bowl of water
. *challah* bread (ask your bakery, but any bread will do)
+ a salt shaker
+ a favorite family meal

The Blessing

As sunset approaches on Friday, I put a small cap called a *yarmulke* on my head. It can also be called a *kippah*, or "skull cap." This is simply a symbol that means I am honoring God's covering of my family. You do not have to wear one, but I do it. As sunset descends, our family gathers, standing around the table, and we "call in" the Sabbath blessing. As with all of these prayers and blessings, there is no specific liturgy to follow. I will give some examples from my family, but you should feel free to create your own personalized blessings and prayers. For our purposes, I will repeat the Sabbath blessing from the last chapter:

> Lord, right now, I welcome the Sabbath peace (*Shabbat shalom*) into my life, my children, my marriage, my finances, my health, and my future.

The Tzedakah Box

In our family, we then put some money in a tzedakah box. The Bible says, *"Train up a child in the way he should go, and when he is old he will not depart from it"* (Proverbs 22:6). As we learned earlier, Jesus taught that the two greatest commandments are to love God and to love your neighbor, that they will know that we belong to Him. We also learned that *tzedakah* is the Hebrew word for "charity" or "justice." In Deuteronomy, it says, "*You shall follow what is altogether just*" (Deuteronomy 16:20). A more accurate translation would be, "Tzedakah, tzedakah you shall pursue."

The tzedakah box is a small receptacle in which the children of the home can donate portions of their allowances to help others. Some of these boxes are hand-carved and ornate; others are made of cardboard. Think of it as a piggy bank for charity. Our family contributes to it every Sabbath, all year long. Then, when someone in the local school or neighborhood is in need, that money is used to help out.

It is an opportunity to teach our children that Scripture says, "*He who has pity on the poor* [anyone in need] *lends to the Lord, and He* [God] *will pay back what he has given*" (Proverbs 19:17). What a great lesson to instill in your children! You'll be amazed at how much of their allowances they will contribute once they experience the blessing of helping others in need. It reminds all of us that it is not enough just to love God; we also must love our neighbor, not just by saying it, but also by living it out and doing something tangible.

> **It is not enough just to love God; we also must love our neighbor.**

Lighting the Candles

Next, the women of the home light the Sabbath candles. You may wonder why women are to do this. As the wife of a rabbi writes, "When a woman lights Shabbat candles she acknowledges that women since Eve have been agents of unity and visionaries of peace, connected to God via the weekly flames they ignite."[11] If there is not a lady in the house, then a man may light it. When I am traveling by myself, for instance, I light the Sabbath candles myself.

Two candles are lit. One is to represent peace; the other is to represent blessing. They remind us that no matter how dark it is outside, when God

---

[11] Leah Kohn, "Women and Shabbat Candles," http://www.torah.org/learning/women/class20.html.

is in your life, His light will always shine. After the candles are lit, the woman (or lighter) waves her hand over them three times to welcome in the power of God, specifically ushering God's light, health, and prosperity into the home and family.

After the candles are lit, the woman puts her hands over her eyes and takes a moment to pray. Rabbis teach us that in this moment, God is so thankful for women that they are closer to Him now than at any other time. The woman who lit the candles then says a prayer for whatever is on her heart. It may be a prayer for her home, marriage, children, or anything else. The moment she opens her eyes, Sabbath has officially begun, and a double portion of anointing is released.

Ministering Angels

The next thing we do is come into agreement in prayer to release the Sabbath angels whom God has assigned to our family and to our children. Hebrews tells us:

> To which of the angels has He ever said: "Sit at My right hand, till I make Your enemies Your footstool"? Are they not all ministering spirits sent forth to minister for those who will inherit salvation?
>
> (Hebrews 1:13–14)

In Jewish tradition, a rabbi is asked, "The Lord created all and blessed the earth, and then He created man, and then He created the Sabbath to bring the blessing to man. What is God doing now?" The rabbi responds, "Since that day, God is building ladders to connect you and me to all of His blessings."

This is a reference to a dream that Jacob had, recorded in Genesis. In the dream, "a ladder was set up on the earth, and its top reached to heaven; and there the angels of God were ascending and descending on it" (Genesis 28:12). Angels are the ministering spirits to those who "inherit salvation." Therefore, as we enter into Sabbath, I will pray:

> Father, we know that Your Word says we have angels that are ministering spirits. I release these angels on all Your people from the north, the south, the east, and the west. I release Your Sabbath

angels. I release the angels of God to lead and guide and protect us. I pray they will be our front guard and our rear guard, and that they will be with our children, our families, and our grandchildren. Walk with us. Father, we give You praise for this revelation, in Jesus' name. Amen.

Blessing the Wife or Mother

The next thing I do is speak a blessing that honors my wife in front of her children and grandchildren. This can be an incredibly meaningful spiritual moment in your marriage and family. As part of your blessing, you may want to read aloud from Proverbs:

Who can find a virtuous wife? For her worth is far above rubies. The heart of her husband safely trusts her; so he will have no lack of gain. She does him good and not evil all the days of her life. She seeks wool and flax, and willingly works with her hands. She is like the merchant ships, she brings her food from afar. She also rises while it is yet night, and provides food for her household, and a portion for her maidservants. She considers a field and buys it; from her profits she plants a vineyard. (Proverbs 31:10–16)

Ladies, this is your scriptural argument that proves women can thrive in business. Women are not just for cooking and cleaning and child rearing; they can also bring prosperity into the home. Let's continue:

She girds herself with strength, and strengthens her arms. She perceives that her merchandise is good, and her lamp does not go out by night. She stretches out her hands to the distaff, and her hand holds the spindle. She extends her hand to the poor, yes, she reaches out her hands to the needy. She is not afraid of snow for her household, for all her household is clothed with scarlet. (verses 17–21)

The word *snow* here refers to death. God covers her family so that no angel of death will come against them, "*for all her household is clothed with scarlet.*" Death can't touch them, because she covers her household each day with blood. In the Old Testament, it was the blood of the lamb from the

Passover. In the New Testament, it is the blood of the Lamb of God, Jesus Christ, that covers us.

She makes tapestry for herself; her clothing is fine linen and purple. Her husband is known in the gates, when he sits among the elders of the land. She makes linen garments and sells them, and supplies sashes for the merchants. (Proverbs 31:22–24)

Many Jews believe this is a reference to the tallit, which is handed down from father to son.

Strength and honor are her clothing; she shall rejoice in time to come. She opens her mouth with wisdom, and on her tongue is the law of kindness. She watches over the ways of her household, and does not eat the bread of idleness. Her children rise up and call her blessed; her husband also, and he praises her: "Many daughters have done well, but you excel them all." Charm is deceitful and beauty is passing, but a woman who fears the LORD, she shall be praised. (verses 25–30)

Men, in this day and age, what an opportunity this is for your children and grandchildren to see you pray for your wife. At this time, I usually ask our family to hold hands around the table as I pray a blessing over Tiz:

Father, I thank You for Tiz. I thank You for bringing her into our lives. I thank You for allowing me to be married to her. I thank You for giving Tiz as the mother of our children. I thank You that she is now nanna, the grandmother of our grandsons and the children who are still to come. Father, I give You praise. What a gift she is to my life and to Your kingdom. What honor she brings on Your name and mine. Father, I cover Tiz with long life, divine health, and Your destiny, because she is not only a light in the world, but also a light in my life and in our family. In Jesus' name, I thank You. Amen.

Blessing the Husband or Father

Next, the wife may pray a blessing over her husband. Once again, these are not hard-and-fast rules. Many families, for one reason or another, may not reflect the traditional "nuclear family" structure. In such cases, be creative and pray as God leads.

Consider Psalm 112, which describes a man of God. As I read it, I begin to get nervous. This is a pretty high standard to live up to. As men, however, it is a worthy goal.

> *Praise the LORD! Blessed is the man who fears the LORD, who delights greatly in His commandments. His descendants will be mighty on earth; the generation of the upright will be blessed. Wealth and riches will be in his house, and his righteousness endures forever. Unto the upright there arises light in the darkness; he is gracious, and full of compassion, and righteous. A good man deals graciously and lends; he will guide his affairs with discretion. Surely he will never be shaken; the righteous will be in everlasting remembrance. He will not be afraid of evil tidings; his heart is steadfast, trusting in the LORD. His heart is established; he will not be afraid, until he sees his desire upon his enemies. He has dispersed abroad, he has given to the poor; his righteousness endures forever; his horn will be exalted with honor. The wicked will see it and be grieved; he will gnash his teeth and melt away; the desire of the wicked shall perish.* (Psalm 112)

In our Sabbath celebration, Tiz will pray something like this:

Father, I thank You for Larry. I thank You for giving him to me as my husband, and as the father of our children, and now as the grandpa of our grandchildren. Father, I thank You for his love, his heart, and his generosity and kindness toward our family. I thank You for this gift that You have given to us, that You have raised him up as a man after Your own heart. Father, I thank You that You will lead him, guide him, and give him Your continual wisdom to lead this family and do all that You have called him to do. Lord, I pray that You will anoint him, endowing him with Your abilities. Equip him inside and out to be the man, the father, the husband, and the leader that You have called him to be. I bless him, in Jesus' name. Amen.

Blessing the Children and Other Family Members

Next, prophesy over your sons, your grandsons, your daughters, and your granddaughters. Jesus promised, *"If two of you agree on earth concerning anything that they ask, it will be done for them by My Father in heaven"* (Matthew 18:19). The goal here is that we would all agree with what God has said and not with what circumstances or people would suggest. The Bible tells us that God sanctified the Sabbath. We already saw the English definition of *sanctify*, but in Hebrew, it denotes a marriage. The notion was that on the Sabbath, we become married to God and His blessings. Therefore, when you bless your children and grandchildren, you are "marrying" them to the promises and blessings of God. What God brings together, no man can put asunder! (See Mark 10:9.)

In keeping with the traditional Sabbath blessing of children, I go to each of my sons, sons-in-law, and grandsons, laying hands on each one and saying, "May he be like Ephraim and Manasseh." This is a traditional Jewish blessing that refers to when Jacob was dying and asked Joseph to bless his two eldest sons in front of their grandfather. Joseph said, *"By you Israel will bless, saying, 'May God make you as Ephraim and as Manasseh!'"* (Genesis 48:20). Ephraim and Manasseh were two sons who served God. They were brothers who did not fight with each other. They didn't split the inheritance, one going God's way and the other going the wrong way. This has remained the Jewish blessing of sons ever since.

> Don't let what you see in the natural affect what you pray for in your spirit.

Rabbis teach that you should whisper something into each son's ear—and don't forget the sons-in-law! We do this even if our sons are not with us, which is the case with most sons who are grown, married, and have families of their own. We still say something positive about them. I say how proud I am of them, how glad I am that they are serving God, and specifically, how glad I am that God brought Brandon into our lives to be the husband of our daughter and the father of our grandchildren. You are prophesying what God says about your kids. If your kids don't know God, prophesy of the day that they will come to Him. Don't let what you see in the natural affect what you pray for in your spirit. God sees your children. He says that you and your family will be saved.

Next, speak over your daughters, daughters-in-law, or granddaughters. Ask that they may be like Rebecca, Sarah, Rachel, and Leah—the mighty women of God in Scripture. These were women who had great anointing, honor, and destiny in God. Whisper something in their ears about how proud you are of them and how honored you are to have them in your life. In our daughter Katie's case, we come in agreement and thank God for the husband we are calling into her life.

In this day and age, you can no longer go out and make a marriage for your daughter, but you can arrange one through prayer in the kingdom of heaven. On the day our daughter Anna was born, we began praying a godly husband into her life. We were already praying for Brandon, her husband, before we knew who he was. The moment our son Luke was born, we started praying for his wife. That means we were praying for Jen, his wife, before she was even born. Although Katie is not married yet, we are praying daily for her husband. We are not leaving our children's or grandchildren's destinies in the hands of this world. We are putting their lives into the hands of God as we come into prophetic agreement over them.

> Father, for our sons, grandsons, and sons-in-law, we thank You that they will be like Ephraim and Manasseh. For our daughters, granddaughters, and daughters-in-law, we thank You that they will be like Rebecca, Rachel, Leah, and Sarah. Father, we release on our children Your divine destiny. We release on them not only divine destiny, but also divine health, long life, and divine prosperity. We release on them Your Spirit. Father, we call our children and our grandchildren in from the north, the south, the east, and the west, and we cover them with Your kingdom. Father, may our children and grandchildren bring honor to Your name; may they bring honor to Your kingdom. May they bring honor to Israel and the people of Israel. May they bring honor to our family name. Father, we break every curse that would try to hinder or delay Your blessing. Father, we thank You that all of our children and all of our grandchildren are covered by the blood of Your Son and

by Your Spirit. We give You all the praise and all the glory in the name of Yesua, in the name of Jesus our Messiah. Amen.

Kiddush

Next is the reciting of *Kiddush* over a cup of wine or grape juice. Once again, the Sabbath is a time of great joy, not solemnity. Wine is a symbol of joy. The first miracle Jesus performed was turning water into fine wine at a wedding celebration. This was a symbol of the ways in which God brings life and wants to turn the world's sorrow into great joy. In traditional Jewish homes, it is recited over a silver goblet, but any type of cup will do. For the Kiddush, you fill your cup to the brim—almost overflowing, because God's joy is overflowing. The joy of the Lord is your strength. (See Nehemiah 8:10.) As we take Kiddush, we praise God for His joy, and we bind everything that wants to steal our joy. Is there something out there that is trying to steal your joy? Is there something out there that is trying to steal the happiness that God paid for by the blood of His Son, Jesus? On the Sabbath, we rebuke it and release the blessings of God into every area of life.

Father, we thank You for the commandment. Father, I rebuke every spirit that is trying to steal the joy out of lives, out of homes, out of marriages, and out of families. Satan, in the name of Jesus, you are bound, you are cast out, and I release unspeakable joy into every family, every marriage, every situation between a father and son, a mother and daughter. I release that joy. I break the spirit that steals finances or brings sickness in an attempt to rob us of our joy. Father, we are reconnected to the promises of God. We are adopted into the covenant family of Abraham, and we receive it, not someday but today, right now. Let all of that joy be released, in Jesus' name. Amen.

Washing Hands

Then, the father or husband washes his hands in a bowl of water on the table. Why do we wash our hands? Water symbolizes divine power and wisdom. We are washing off the limits of this world. The ceilings in our lives are removed so that God might "*do exceedingly abundantly above all that we ask or think, according to the power that works in us*" (Ephesians 3:20). As you wash your hands, God makes your way straight. He will give you divine wisdom and power so that everything you put your hands to will prosper. (See Deuteronomy 28:8.) It doesn't matter who you are. It doesn't matter where you are living. You are washing off the limitations of this world. We may be living in

> **We may be living in this world, but the limitations of this world are not on any of us.**

this world, but the limitations of this world are not on any of us because we have been born again and redeemed by the blood of Jesus Christ. We wash our hands because this is our part in our covenant with God.

The *Challah* Bread

As we move into the Sabbath meal, we first partake of the *challah* bread (pronounced "halla"). This type of bread can be found in most bakeries these days. It looks like a loaf of bread that has been braided. Of course, if you can't find actual challah, any type of bread will suffice. The challah bread is symbolic of prosperity. Let me tell you something: prosperity is not bad. Greed is bad; prosperity is a blessing and is of God. Just as your wishes for your own children's prosperity are a noble and honorable desire, God's desire is for His children to thrive and prosper.

The challah bread has a covering—usually a plate or a towel—on the top and bottom. This symbolizes the time when God was giving Israel manna in the desert. Classic rabbinical teaching suggests that the manna in the desert had a layer of dew on top of and below it. According to the rabbis, this was a supernatural covering—a supernatural touch of God.

The dew added flavor. Can you imagine eating the same thing every day? Thankfully, our God is not only concerned about the quality of eternity but also about the flavor of our lives on earth. The psalmist wrote, "*Taste and see that the LORD is good*" (Psalm 34:8). Jesus said, "*I have come that they may have life, and that they may have it more abundantly*" (John 10:10).

Knowing God is not bland. Knowing God has great flavor. Knowing God has great excitement. When I first became a Christian, I thought God was going to take life away. What I discovered was that He did not come to take my joy but to bring joy into my life.

The layer of dew on top of the manna was for protection. The nation of Israel was in the desert, where the sun was intense and would devour anything left uncovered. Likewise, God will not only bless you, but He will also rebuke the devourer. The dew covered the manna to protect the Israelites' blessing so that nothing in this world could steal it away.

Just before the Sabbath meal, take the challah bread and lift it up. For the Jews, this is a remembrance of God's provision in the desert. For the Christian, it is a reminder of Jesus when He said, *"And I, if I am lifted up from the earth, will draw all peoples to Myself"* (John 12:32). It is more than Jesus being lifted up onto the cross. It is the resurrection power of God being released and raising Christ from the dead. It is the miracle of Christ's ascension into heaven, where He goes to prepare a place for us. Through the challah bread, God releases to us the power of His resurrection. Therefore, we say what is called the *hamotzi* over the bread. Lift it in the air and say,

> Our Father, who brings bread from the earth for our provision, I receive a double portion of Your blessing on my life in every area, in the name of Jesus, in the name of Yeshua, our Messiah. Amen.

Sprinkling the Salt

Next, you take a pinch of salt and sprinkle it on the bread. In the temple, the high priest would always sprinkle salt on the burnt offerings. You are the "high priest" of your home, and everything you touch is blessed of God—ordained to have His anointing on it. You and I may be in this world, but we are not limited to this world. Sprinkle the salt and say,

> Sickness will not come into our home. Poverty, divorce, and drugs will not enter our home. We rebuke it, and we receive *Shabbat shalom*—the Sabbath peace. Nothing is missing, and nothing is broken here.

The Sabbath Menu

Remember the words of the rabbi at the beginning of this chapter: "It is never all or nothing." There is no wrong way to welcome in the Sabbath. From here on, the menu of your meal really does not matter. There is no need for you to experiment with traditional Jewish dishes such as gefilte fish, matzo balls, brisket, and kugel—unless you are curious, of course. It is probably better to serve dishes your family enjoys and associates with meaningful times together. Have pizza, if you like. Remember, *"Let no one judge you in food or in drink, or regarding a festival or a new moon or sabbaths"* (Colossians 2:16).

> "It is never all or nothing." There is no wrong way to welcome in the Sabbath.

What's important is that every Friday evening, as the sun begins to set, you gather your family together. If they are not with you, then speak blessings over them as you welcome in the Sabbath and bask in that special time of the Lord—a time He has set aside for you.

Do we have to do it? No.

Do we get to do it? Yes.

Here is the testimony of one couple at New Beginnings who have discovered the blessings of God through their Jewish roots:

Sabbath Blessings Released

We started our journey at New Beginnings just four months after the church opened in Dallas. We came from a church where many of the teachings were of hellfire and damnation. We were taught that God loved us, but if we got out of the will of God, He would do something to us or our loved ones to get our attention. We were struggling financially and had lost almost everything we owned. I was battling depression and had low self-esteem. My husband, James, struggled with anger issues. As an interracial couple, we also had to deal with the ugliness of racism, both from our families and from the outside world.

Despite everything, we still loved each other, we loved our families, and most of all, we loved our God. We knew that there had to be more to God and His Word than what we were being taught.

Soon, we discovered Pastor Larry's teaching about the Jewish roots of Christianity. We attended a conference where we heard refreshing and uplifting messages of how much God loves us. We were able to address the curses of containment and failure that were working in our lives. We also learned about Shabbat. Now, every Friday, we keep the Sabbath, welcoming in the Spirit of God at this appointed time and speaking His Word and promises over each other, our families, and our business. We end our week on a positive thought, and we begin our week on a positive thought, thanking God for His goodness. God's Word has become alive and exciting. The manifestation of God working in our lives has been miraculous.

We have discovered firsthand the truth that God can do in your life only what you allow Him to do through your understanding of Him. For us, our biggest growth has been in the area of finances. Our first tithe to the church was $126. We had an electrical contracting business that was bogged down in debt. Our business started thriving.

Each year, as our knowledge of God's Word has increased, so has our giving. Last year, we were able, by God's grace and provision, to give over $250,000 in tithes, offerings, and mitzvahs.

The understanding of our Jewish roots, especially keeping and remembering the Shabbat, has strengthened our marriage by bringing us into the kind of close unity we had never known in our twenty-three years of marriage. The ugliness of racism has been replaced with love and forgiveness. Depression has been replaced with joy and fulfillment. Worthlessness has been replaced with a sense of purpose and destiny. Anger has been replaced with peace and strength. I cannot begin to explain all the ways in which understanding the Jewish roots of our faith has enriched our lives. It has truly been a life-changing experience.

—Rita Evans

Get Married to Your Blessings

The rabbis teach that the Sabbath is the hub of the universe. It is the first rung on the ladder of knowing God. God created the heavens and the earth. He looked at everything that was and said it was good. Then He said, in effect, "Now, I am going to create man, and I am going to create *menuhah*—a rest and a blessing. I am going to sanctify this day. I am going to 'marry' My children with their blessings because it is a Father's good pleasure to give them My kingdom."

Sabbath Rest: A Breath of Fresh Air

What does "returning to our Jewish roots" mean to us? It means undergoing a change that is evident in every area of our lives—a change that is felt deep within our souls! As we began to learn the importance of understanding our Jewish roots, it was as if scales fell from our eyes. We had studied the Bible and attended church for many years, but what we learned and are continuing to learn from Pastors Larry and Tiz has been life changing in all that we think and do.

We have learned to read the Bible through the eyes of the Jews who wrote it as opposed to gaining our understanding through Western Christian interpretation. We now have a deeper understanding of who Jesus was, His way of life, and His customs. We understand that Jesus honored all the feasts, and, in particular, we have learned to enter into the blessing and joy of Shabbat.

Oh, Shabbat! If only we could have experienced you from childhood! When we light the Shabbat candles on Friday evening, our home is filled with the love of God. Honoring Shabbat has blessed us in ways we could only have dreamed were possible. It is as if God has knitted and meshed our spirits together and given our marriage a peace and unity never experienced before. We love this special time. We now understand the power and love that has been so beautifully woven into the fabric of our lives.

When we pray and bless our children during this special time, we expect good things to happen. Pastor Larry taught us that our Father adds His "super" to our "natural"—and it is true! We pray for our business, for the past week, and for the coming week. Monumental breakthroughs have occurred, and it seems we always receive good news on Shabbat. We have overcome obstacles and fought battles, but we know that as we light our candles for Shabbat, as our Father hears our prayers, and as we enter into His rest, the battles are won!

—Jack and Patricia Roubinek

Keep and remember the Sabbath. Enter into the rest your Father has created especially for you. Enter into a covenant *relationship* with God, and receive all the blessings of His kingdom.

God bless you.

Shabbat shalom.

The Seven Feasts

S ome of you may be wondering, *If we already believe in Jesus as our Messiah, why do we have to remember Jewish holidays?*

Once again, my answer is: we don't have to; we get to!

We don't *have* to remember Christ's resurrection on Easter Sunday, but isn't it good for us to do so? Doesn't it make us better as Christians? As Americans, each Fourth of July, we teach our children the values on which our nation was founded. We teach them to say the Pledge of Allegiance. We teach them to honor the veterans who sacrificed their lives so that our nation can be free. These activities are not a legal requirement for being Americans, but by celebrating and remembering, don't we become better Americans? We remember that freedom is not free. We celebrate the fact that all men are created equal. There is something meaningful and beneficial in remembering and celebrating our heritage.

In Scripture, there are seven different feasts that God gave His people. Isn't that amazing? There aren't six or eight, but seven—the biblical number of perfection or completion. All seven feasts, without exception, point directly and prophetically to Jesus Christ. Because of this, I believe it is still important that Christians, as well as Jews, observe them. They are a portal to some of the richest and most powerful of God's blessings.

In the spring is Passover, the day that the lamb was slain and the blood was put on the doorpost, just as the blood of Jesus was also shed on Passover.

Passover is on the first and second days of the seven-day **Feast of Unleavened Bread,** a remembrance of Israel passing through the Red Sea to receive their sustenance from God. It also represents a removal of sin, or leaven, from our homes and our lives.

At the end of Passover is the **Feast of Firstfruits,** in which a sheaf of barley was brought into the temple and presented to the Lord. This offering pointed to Jesus' resurrection, as Paul said, *"Now Christ is risen from the dead, and has become the firstfruits of those who have fallen asleep"* (1 Corinthians 15:20).

In the summer, fifty days later, is the **Feast of Pentecost,** because Moses received the Ten Commandments on Mount Sinai fifty days after Israel passed through the Red Sea. Similarly, fifty days after Jesus was raised from the dead, His followers received the Holy Spirit—the Christian Pentecost. Both were received with thunder, lightning, and streaks of fire.

In the fall are the Feasts of Rosh Hashanah, Yom Kippur, and Sukkot. **Rosh Hashanah** means "new year" or "the beginning year." As you will discover, this is, for Christians, a symbol of the rapture—not the second coming, but the time when God will judge the nations and take the righteous, living and dead, out of this world.

The **Feast of Yom Kippur**—or the Day of Atonement—is the day God forgives the sins of Israel. For Christians, this points to the seven years of tribulation when those who have been left behind must accept Jesus as their Messiah before His second coming to set up His kingdom on earth.

Sukkot—or the **Feast of Tabernacles**—is the millennium reign of Christ on earth as God lives with—*tabernacles with*—His people.

All of these feasts and their prophetic meanings were given to man in the Torah, God's path. They were, and are, essential in living out our purpose on earth of loving God and loving others.

And the LORD spoke to Moses, saying, "Speak to the children of Israel, and say to them: 'The feasts of the LORD, which you shall proclaim to be holy convocations, these are My feasts....These are the feasts of the LORD, holy convocations which you shall proclaim at their appointed times.'" (Leviticus 23:1–2, 4)

These feasts are for everyone, not just the Jewish people. They are for all of those who have been *"grafted in"* (Romans 11:17).

 * *See appendix for chart detailing overview of Jewish feasts, their dates, and ways to celebrate.*

9

The Feasts of Passover, Unleavened Bread, and Firstfruits

For our purposes, I am going to combine the first three feasts into the week that we call Passover. Again, I'll repeat my disclaimer that these feasts are not about legalism but about a releasing of God's blessings for those who know and understand God's Word and its meaning.

The Feast of Unleavened Bread

Passover occurs on the first, and often also on the second, night of the seven-day period called the Feast of Unleavened Bread. For the Jews, unleavened flatbread reminds them that their deliverance happened so quickly that there was no time to bake proper bread for their journey. It's also a reminder of the manna God provided in the desert.

In Hebrew, *leaven* is also symbolic for the impulses of an evil heart. For Jews, leaven is representative of sin in our lives. In traditional Jewish homes, there is no leaven allowed during these seven days, during which they eat only Matzah and no bread that has risen. Before Passover begins, Jewish women meticulously go through their homes, getting rid of all food containing leaven. Sometimes it is consumed in the weeks leading up to Passover, and sometimes it is given away to local food banks. Some Jewish congregations allow a room in the house to store all leaven, and this room is sealed off beginning on Passover. Once all leaven has been removed from the kitchen, all surfaces and appliances are then thoroughly scrubbed to do away with any trace or crumb. Besides its spiritual meaning, it also becomes a great time of spring cleaning. In some homes, pieces of regular bread are hidden around the house as Passover begins. The children are to hunt for them, find them, and remove them from the home. It's a game they play, teaching the lesson that God is cleansing the house and family from all impurities.

The Feast of Passover

To understand Passover and its essential connection with Christianity, let us go back to Jesus' final days on earth with His beloved disciples.

> *Then came the Day of Unleavened Bread, when the Passover must be killed. And He sent Peter and John, saying, "Go and prepare the Passover for us, that we may eat." So they said to Him, "Where do You want us to prepare?" And He said to them, "Behold, when you have entered the city, a man will meet you carrying a pitcher of water; follow him into the house which he enters. Then you shall say to the master of the house, 'The Teacher says to you, "Where is the guest room where I may eat the Passover with My disciples?"' Then he will show you a large, furnished upper room; there make ready." So they went and found it just as He had said to them, and they prepared the Passover. When the hour had come, He sat down, and the twelve apostles with Him. Then He said to them, "With fervent desire I have desired to eat this Passover with you before I suffer."* (Luke 22:7–15)

When we celebrate what's called the Lord's Supper, or Communion, we need to understand that when Jesus gave us this remembrance, He was not just hanging out and enjoying some barbeque with the boys. He was celebrating Passover. I guess I always knew that—after all, it's right there in Scripture—but it never really hit me. I just thought that since Jesus knew He was going to die, He gathered the guys together for a final shindig, knowing that bad news was better received on a full stomach. I assumed that when the meal was over, He grabbed whatever was on the table—a loaf of bread and a cup of wine—to give them a little illustration, a new teaching for them to follow and share with others. That is not at all what happened.

Jesus was following the teachings of God, which said that at this time every year, they were to celebrate Passover. It was clearly stipulated in the Torah:

*And the L*ORD *spoke to Moses, saying, "...The feasts of the L*ORD*, which you shall proclaim to be holy convocations, these are My feasts.... On the fourteenth day of the first month at twilight is the Lord's Passover."* (Leviticus 23:1–2, 5)

For first-century Jews, Passover was not optional. It was not a national holiday like Labor Day, which you are free to observe or ignore. These feasts of the Lord were *"holy convocations."* They were not simply a nod toward tradition. I've met Jews who keep the Sabbath only out of tradition. That's fine, but there's no power in it. Likewise, there are Christians who take part in baptism and Communion only out of tradition, but there's no power in that, either. There is no power in anything we do simply because it is some kind of "religious formula." The apostle Paul referred to this when he wrote of men *"having a form* [formula] *of godliness but denying its power"* (2 Timothy 3:5). When we teach these things, it's not an attempt to perform a *ceremony.* It has nothing to do with the ceremony.

For example, I have what the Jews call a *mezuzah* on every doorpost of my house. A mezuzah is a little plaque inscribed with words from the Shema, beginning with, "Hear, O Israel: the Lord is our God, the Lord is One." (See Deuteronomy 6:4.) I do this because I read that God said, in effect, "Take My words and *'write them on the doorposts of your house'"* (Deuteronomy 6:9). When I walk into my house, I'm fighting the devil and trying to bring the Word of God and the victory of Jesus into peoples' lives. When I see that mezuzah, it reminds me that I don't live by what I feel or by what I'm going through. I live by the promises of God. I'm blessed going in and blessed going out. (See Deuteronomy 28:6.)

There is absolutely nothing supernatural about putting a mezuzah on your doorpost. It's not some kind of good luck charm. Everything God gives us is to remind us of His goodness. When we keep Shabbat, it is to remind us of His goodness, because God gave us the fourth commandment: remember the Sabbath and keep it holy. It is not magic or mystical but a practical reminder that realigns me, reflects the goodness of God, and celebrates His presence in our home.

> **Everything God gives us is to remind us of His goodness.**

The Passover meal is also called the *Seder*, a Hebrew word meaning "order" or "arrangement," because there is a fixed order to the evening that is followed by Jews around the world. Unlike many Jewish celebrations and practices, the Seder meal is to be shared in the home by family and friends, not celebrated in a synagogue. It is a participatory celebration and an integral part of Jewish faith and identity. It retells the story of God's deliverance of Israel from slavery in Egypt and of their trek through the desert to the Promised Land. It is a time of praise and thanksgiving for their God-given redemption and liberation. Because of the participatory nature of the night, as well as the intergenerational involvement, it is one of the primary ways that Jewish faith and tradition are passed from father to son and mother to daughter.

The Hebrew word for *Passover* is *Pesach*, which also means "to be protected under the wings." This is why, as He approached Jerusalem, Jesus said, "*O Jerusalem, Jerusalem....How often I wanted to gather your children together, as a hen gathers her brood under her wings*" (Luke 13:34). Remember, Jesus was a Jewish rabbi speaking to a Jewish audience who knew what these things meant. Jesus was saying, "I will cover you. I will stand by My blood in front of your door, and the enemy will be forbidden from entering ever again."

On the night Christians call Good Friday (Thursday evening after sundown), Jesus sat with his "family," his closest followers, in an upper room just hours before His crucifixion and took part in the Seder meal on the first night of Passover. This was no accident or coincidence. It was all part of the plan. As they shared in the Passover meal, Jesus bluntly told them that He was about to give up His life. He was letting the world know, in no uncertain terms, "I *am* the Passover Lamb."

The Lamb of God

Why did God instruct His people to always remember the Passover? To Israel, the Passover lamb was a physical redemption. God literally passed over His people, brought affliction on the nation of Egypt, and led them out of years of slavery. To the "new Israel"—the "grafted in" Israel—it is both a physical and a spiritual redemption. As Christians, we have always been taught that Jesus was the Lamb of God. At Jesus' baptism, John the Baptist said, *"Behold! The Lamb of God who takes away the sin of the world!"* (John 1:29).

When we celebrate Passover, understanding that Jesus is the Lamb of God, the Bible says that we are to sit down from generation to generation and explain to our children exactly what is going on.

> *And you shall observe this thing as an ordinance for you and your sons forever....And it shall be, when your children say to you, "What do you mean by this service?" that you shall say, "It is the Passover sacrifice of the LORD, who passed over the houses of the children of Israel in Egypt when He struck the Egyptians and delivered our households."*
> (Exodus 12:24, 26–27)

There is something special about oral teaching. The more you teach something, the more it becomes ingrained in the listener. What seems like a ritual suddenly becomes a revelation. Thus, at the same time every year, God asks us to remember Passover around the same time we celebrate Easter. Now don't get me wrong. I love chocolate Easter eggs as much as the next guy, but if our kids know more about bunnies that lay chocolate eggs than they know about the Passover Lamb, we as the children of God are missing something.

That All Might Come

> *For I will pass through the land of Egypt on that night, and will strike all the firstborn in the land of Egypt, both man and beast; and against all the gods of Egypt I will execute judgment: I am the LORD.*
> (Exodus 12:12)

While you celebrate Passover, one of the activities is to dip your finger in one of the cups of wine or grape juice, representing the blood of the lamb, and sprinkle it on the Seder plate ten times, once for each of the plagues that came on Egypt. According to rabbinical teaching, your finger represents the finger of God. The blood brought great destruction and death to the people of Egypt. As Christians, we are excited about being raptured one day.

We need to realize, however, that when God takes His people out of this earth, it will take all the goodness away, as well. Just as plagues were released throughout Egypt, Satan will be unleashed upon the earth. There will be disease, wars, pestilence, and all kinds of evil things unchecked upon the land. When we are gone, it will be at a great cost to the people left behind. As Christians, perhaps we don't think enough about that. We may just think, *Hey, when I'm gone, I'm gone. See ya. Wouldn't want to be ya. I win; you lose.*

> **We need to be doing everything we can to fulfill the purpose of God in our lives and reach this world with the good news of Jesus Christ.**

God, however, doesn't see it that way. I don't care if the person is a Jew or a Gentile or a Muslim or a Hindu or an atheist, God loves all of mankind, and it will break His heart when He comes back for us. That's why we need to be doing everything we can to fulfill the purpose of God in our lives and reach this world with the good news of Jesus Christ.

This is why God instructed His people to keep the Sabbath and to celebrate Passover and Yom Kippur and Rosh Hashanah. Through all of these feasts, God is teaching us to remain focused. I believe in prosperity and want to see all of God's children prosper. I believe in healing and want to see all of God's children made whole. I believe in all the gifts of the Spirit, but sometimes we can get sidetracked going after this gift or that gift when our main purpose here on earth is to love the Lord our God with all our hearts and to love our neighbors as ourselves. God is not interested in rituals; He wants us to remember what life is all about.

> *Now the blood shall be a sign for you on the houses where you are. And when I see the blood, I will pass over you; and the plague shall not be on you to destroy you when I strike the land of Egypt. So this day shall be to you a memorial; and you shall keep it as a feast to the LORD throughout your generations. You shall keep it as a feast by an everlasting ordinance.* (Exodus 12:13–14)

Passover is an everlasting ordinance or covenant between God and His children. This is not only about our salvation; it is also about keeping our focus on His goodness. It's about how He loves you and desires to bless you, but it is also about how you are to love your neighbor as you love yourself. These things will always keep you in alignment with the purpose and the goodness of God.

The Seder Meal

Preparing for the Seder is important if the evening is to run smoothly, especially since many Christians have never participated in one, let alone planned it. The preparations are not complicated, but they need to be given some consideration ahead of time. It is usually wise to begin planning and gathering materials several days before the actual date, since some of the items may need to be specially ordered. Careful thought and planning ahead of time will make the experience more enjoyable for those leading and attending the Seder.

The Seder Plate

One item you will want to find is a Seder plate. It is not mandatory, but it will make the celebration easier. These are available at Jewish supply stores or local synagogues, if you live near a Jewish population, or they can be ordered online. These are decorative plates with five or six separated sections. These sections are for specific items that will be used in the Passover service, such as:

1. a hard-boiled egg, traditionally a brown or roasted egg.

2. *charoset*, a paste made from apples or dates, nuts, honey, and cinnamon, representing mortar; many charoset recipes can be found in books or online.

3. a sprig of parsley.

4. *maror*, or bitter herbs; traditionally, a piece of raw horseradish root is symbolically placed on the Seder plate, but it is not actually used in the service since grated horseradish is used; a teaspoon of horseradish sauce can be used on the plate instead.

5. a small roasted shank bone of lamb, which can be found at any butcher counter.

6. a leaf of romaine lettuce for plates with six compartments (some Seder plates hold only five items).

Setting the Table

Besides the Seder plate, you will need the following items placed at the head of the table:

+ four clear goblets or wine glasses filled with wine or grape juice,

+ two candlesticks,

+ three pieces of flat matzah bread placed on a napkin-covered plate or basket, each separated by a single white napkin with the top one also covered by a napkin,

+ three clear finger bowls: one with salt water, one with extra charoset, and one with horseradish sauce,

+ pitcher of water and bowl for hand washing,

+ a hand towel, and

+ the order of service and text, called the *Haggadah*.

Each guest for the Seder would then have the following items preset at his or her table setting:

+ a dinner plate,

+ a napkin,

+ a wine glass,

+ a fork and spoon,

+ a water glass,

+ a sprig of fresh parsley,

+ a full piece of matzah bread,

+ a small bowl of salt water,

+ extra towels if all the men will wash their hands, and

+ a copy of the Seder Haggadah.

The Seder Service

I am going to go through a sample Seder service. Although there are certain sections that are traditionally scripted, like the Sabbath celebration, you should feel free to make the prayers, blessings, and even the telling of the Exodus story your own.

We welcome in Passover in much the same way as we welcomed in the Sabbath. At sunset, the woman of the home lights the candles (but again, this can be done by anyone) and prays the blessing. Here is a typical blessing:

> Father, as we light these candles for Passover, we declare this to be a holy time set aside for You. We ask You to shed Your light, Your miracles, all of Your promises, Your goodness, and Your joy into our lives, families, and homes during this special time. We love You so much, in the name of Yeshua. Amen.

The Kiddush

When most Christians take Communion, they drink from only one cup. The Seder meal, however, and therefore the table that Jesus shared with His followers, has four different cups for the wine. Each one of them has a tremendous spiritual meaning for our lives—of meaning that is found in the Torah:

> *Therefore say to the children of Israel: "I am the* Lord; *I will **bring you out** from under the burdens of the Egyptians, I will **rescue you** from their bondage, and I will **redeem you** with an outstretched arm and with great judgments. I will **take you** as My people, and I will be your God."* (Exodus 6:6–7, emphasis added)

In this passage are four distinct promises or blessings that God gave Israel. Each one is represented by a cup at the Seder dinner.

1. I will **bring you out** from under your burdens.

2. I will **rescue you** from bondage.

3. I will **redeem you** by My hand.

4. I will **take you** as My people and be your God.

Thus, throughout the Seder service, the leader drinks from four different cups.

The Cup of Sanctification

This first cup is to remind us that through the blood of Jesus, our Passover Lamb, our sins have been washed away. *"Though your sins are like scarlet, they shall be as white as snow"* (Isaiah 1:18). We cannot let the devil condemn us and tell us we aren't worthy because, although we may have been sinners, we are not sinners any longer but children of the living God.

In most Communion services, the bread is distributed before the cup. But in the book of Luke, Jesus first lifted up the cup, because, once again, they were celebrating Passover, as we are. *"Then He took the cup, and gave thanks, and said, 'Take this and divide it among yourselves'"* (Luke 22:17).

Therefore, we lift up the cup of sanctification and say a blessing over it:

Father, I thank You for Your commandment of releasing the joy and the blessing as we receive the cup of sanctification. Let it remind us that we are the righteousness of God. Because of our Passover Lamb and the blood of Jesus, every one of us has the right to go before the throne of God to have our prayers not only heard but answered, in Jesus' name. Amen.

All then drink from this cup—or the leader drinks from this cup, and everyone else drinks from his own cup.

Hand Washing

As on the Sabbath, the men at the table wash their hands. This is done with a large basin of water, much like a baptismal. When the apostle Peter was asked what must be done to receive the Holy Spirit, he said, *"Repent, and let every one of you be baptized in the name of Jesus Christ for the remission of sins; and you shall receive the gift of the Holy Spirit"* (Acts 2:38). When he said *"be baptized,"* however, he used the word *baptizma*. Literally, this means "to baptize yourself." As you wash hands, symbolic of baptism, you are breaking every curse that blocks God's blessings from coming into your life and family. You are now reborn by the baptism, by the washing of the water according to the Word (see Ephesians 5:26), so that God can do something spiritual in your life. You don't have to, but as I wash, I like to say something like this:

> Every curse, every family curse, is broken and reversed in every area of my life and this home, in Jesus' name.

> As you wash your hands, you are breaking every curse that blocks God's blessings from coming into your life and family.

The Sprig of Parsley

On the Passover plate, as well as on each of the participants' plates, is a sprig of parsley. When you pick up that parsley, it is to remind you that when the spirit of death was approaching, the people of Israel dipped their hyssop branches into the blood of the lamb—the lamb without spot or blemish—and applied the blood to the doorposts of their homes. God reminds us that no matter what is coming in this world—be it cancer, divorce, poverty, or anything else—it will come to your door, see the blood, and know that it cannot enter that house. As Christians, we need to be applying the blood of Christ every day. I tell you, I will never see parsley the same way ever again. They may put it on my plate at a restaurant as a garnish, but when I see it, I will always be reminded of Christ's blood.

Dip the parsley into the salt water and take a bite. The salt is a representation of the bitter tears we shed before we were delivered—before we knew the Son of God, the King of Kings and Lord of Lords. Our tears were not wasted, however, for Psalm 56:8 tells us that God actually collects each tear we shed: "*You number my wanderings; put my tears into Your bottle; are they not in Your book?*"

The Unleavened Bread

Now, the leader takes the basket or plate with the three pieces of matzah bread and removes the middle piece. Take the middle piece and break it. Most Jews will tell you that they don't know why this is done; it's just the way they do it. I can tell you that there are three pieces of bread for the Father, Son, and Holy Spirit. The middle one is removed and broken. When Jesus broke the bread in the upper room, He was at this point in the Seder service.

> And He took bread, gave thanks and broke it, and gave it to them, saying, "This is My body which is given for you; do this in remembrance of Me." (Luke 22:19)

How powerful this is, not just as some new practice that Jesus was demonstrating for His followers, but also as part of their Passover celebration—something His disciples had participated in since their earliest memories of childhood—now being fulfilled in their presence!

Once the middle matzah is broken, one half is put back in between the two complete pieces—I refer to it as being put into the tomb. The other half is set aside. In traditional Jewish homes, this half is broken into pieces, one for each child. The children then close their eyes, and the pieces are "hidden" around the room. After the Seder meal, the children will conduct a hunt for these pieces. When they bring back a piece, they are given a small prize or piece of candy. As Christians, we know this is because whoever finds Jesus in this life is greatly rewarded!

Telling the Story—The Haggadah

Now, we come to the retelling of the Exodus story. This can be done briefly or with great detail—it's up to you. For our purposes, I will tell it as I like to do it. It begins, however, by having children ask the traditional questions that have been asked for centuries. The greatest way to get someone else to learn is to have that person ask a question. At this point in the Seder service, the children ask the father of the family four questions. If no children are present, four adults can be assigned the questions. In response, the father retells the Passover story. The four questions can be read from the Haggadah provided:

Child 1: Father, why is this night different from all other nights?

Child 2: Why on other nights do we eat leavened bread, but on this night we eat only unleavened bread?

Child 3: Why on other nights do we eat all kinds of vegetables, but on this night we eat only bitter herbs?

Child 4: Why on other nights do we eat meat that is baked or grilled or marinated, but on this night we eat only roasted meat?

The rabbi, or the father of the house, then tells the story that begins with Abraham—the first Jew—who received the revelation that there are not multiple gods but one true God. Everything started with Abraham. This is why Paul said, *"Those who are of faith are blessed with believing Abraham"* (Galatians 3:9). Abraham's line continued to his son, Isaac, who fathered Jacob, who then fathered Joseph.

Joseph was favored over all his brothers, who grew jealous and sold him into slavery. Eventually, Joseph ended up in Egypt in the house of Potiphar. Everywhere Joseph went, he found great favor from God. He was so blessed that from prison and slavery, he rose into the number two position in Egypt behind only Pharaoh himself. With famine raging in Canaan, Joseph's family and, eventually, all of what would become Israel went to Egypt, where, thanks to Joseph's favor, there was plenty to eat. What many people forget is that when Israel first landed in Egypt, they weren't slaves. They were businesspeople and community and government leaders.

Eventually, however, the pharaoh of Joseph's day died, and a new pharaoh took the throne who did not realize that the reason Egypt was so blessed was because of the children of God. He looked at the Jews and realized that they were growing more numerous and wealthier than the population of Egypt. He proceeded to take everything they had and forced them into slavery, where they spent the next four hundred years making bricks and building structures for the Egyptians.

Eventually, the Jews cried out to God, and He sent them Moses, who went before Pharaoh with a message from the God of Israel: *"Let My people go"* (Exodus 5:1). The Bible says that Pharaoh hardened his heart, so God sent ten plagues on the nation of Egypt. These plagues were sent to demonstrate that the God of Israel was stronger than Egypt's false gods. The Nile River was one of their gods, so God turned it to blood. The sun was one of their gods, so God caused it to go dark. The harvest was one of their gods, so God sent locusts to destroy it. Each plague wiped out a supposed strength of the Egyptian nation.

The last plague sent to Egypt was the killing of all of their firstborn sons. If you don't understand the Bible, this probably seems a bit harsh. It doesn't seem like something that would be within the nature of our loving Father. We need to remember that God's Word says, *"Do not be deceived, God is not mocked; for whatever a man sows, that he will also reap"* (Galatians 6:7). As a baby, Moses was found in a basket in the Nile by one of Pharaoh's daughters, and he was raised as one of the royal household. The very reason, however, that Moses' Jewish mother had put him in that basket was because the pharaoh had ordered the killing of *all* Jewish sons, not just the firstborn. (See Exodus 1:22.) God saved Moses so that he could later go the pharaoh and bring about Israel's redemption by killing all of Egypt's firstborn sons. Pharaoh was reaping exactly what he had sowed. God didn't bring that plague upon Pharaoh; Pharaoh's own actions brought it upon himself.

After each of the first six plagues, Pharaoh hardened his heart against Moses and his message from God. From the seventh plague on, however, the Bible says that God hardened Pharaoh's heart. Perhaps you don't think this sounds fair, but God knew that if Pharaoh consented and restored all of Israel's wealth and status, they probably would have stayed right where they were—in Egypt. God knew that they had to get out of Egypt and into the Promised Land, because mankind needed a Savior, and the only place He could be born was in the land of Israel.

As the final deadly plague loomed over Egypt, God pulled Moses and Aaron aside and gave them instructions about what would be Israel's ultimate deliverance out of Egypt and out of slavery:

> Now the LORD spoke to Moses and Aaron in the land of Egypt, saying, "This month shall be your beginning of months; it shall be the first month of the year to you. Speak to all the congregation of Israel, saying: 'On the tenth day of this month every man shall take for himself

*a lamb, according to the house of his father, a lamb for a household....
Your lamb shall be without blemish, a male of the first year....Then the
whole assembly of the congregation of Israel shall kill it at twilight. And
they shall take some of the blood and put it on the two doorposts and
on the lintel of the houses where they eat it. Then they shall eat the flesh
on that night; roasted in fire, with unleavened bread and with bitter
herbs they shall eat it....And thus you shall eat it: with a belt on your
waist, your sandals on your feet, and your staff in your hand. So you
shall eat it in haste. It is the Lord's Passover. For I will pass through
the land of Egypt on that night, and will strike all the firstborn in the
land of Egypt, both man and beast; and against all the gods of Egypt I
will execute judgment: I am the* LORD*. Now the blood shall be a sign
for you on the houses where you are. And when I see the blood, I will
pass over you; and the plague shall not be on you to destroy you when I
strike the land of Egypt.'"* (Exodus 12:1–3, 5–8, 11–13)

After the horror of the tenth plague, a broken Pharaoh ordered the
Jews to leave his cursed country. Proverbs says that *"the wealth of the sinner
is stored up for the righteous"* (Proverbs 13:22). Was that ever true in this
case! Israel marched out of slavery with all of Egypt's wealth, not out of
punishment, but because Egypt owed them four hundred years of back
wages!

The Cup of Deliverance

The second cup, therefore, is the cup of deliverance. Through the blood
of Jesus, not only are we forgiven, but the Bible also says,

*If a man has committed a sin deserving of death, and he is put to death,
and you hang him on a tree...he who is hanged is accursed of God.*
(Deuteronomy 21:22–23)

This verse is then quoted by Paul:

*Christ has redeemed us from the curse of the law, having become a curse
for us (for it is written, "Cursed is everyone who hangs on a tree").*
(Galatians 3:13)

Jesus did not die merely for our sin. If all He had to do was die, He could have died from stoning, flogging, or from being thrown off a cliff, which was a Jewish punishment. Jesus, however, had to get to the cross because He didn't just die for our sin; He died to break every curse off of our lives. That's why He is able to break the curses of poverty, racism, anger, and addiction. He doesn't just forgive you; He gives you a brand-new life free of the curses from your past.

> **Jesus didn't just die for our sin; He died to break every curse off of our lives.**

Before drinking from the cup of deliverance, the leader lifts it up and dips his finger into the cup, which represents the blood of the Passover Lamb—the blood of Jesus. Using that finger, he then puts ten drops onto the Passover plate and leaves them there. This is to remind us that God has delivered us from our curses. Ten is for the ten plagues sent on Egypt. Although we have been delivered, it is also a reminder that there is a world out there we need to reach for Jesus Christ. Our freedom is never complete as long as there is someone else in bondage. We're not here just to go to church; we're here to change the world because Jesus first did that for us. Now, we raise the cup of deliverance and say a blessing:

> Father, we thank You that not only are our sins washed away, but also that we are born again. We thank You that every curse is broken. The weeds that choke out the blessings have been killed. Now, Father, bring us the harvest, in Jesus' name. Amen.

The Second Hand Washing

It's now time for all the men to wash their hands a second time by dipping their hands into the bowl of water. We are reminding ourselves that we are cleansed from all the impurities and limitations of this world. Jesus was baptized in the Jordan River, not to be part of any church, but as a sign that we are cleansed from the limits of this world. It is a sign that, because we are born again, we may be *in* this world, but we are no longer *of* this world. In the washing with water, we are released spiritually through the kingdom of God. We break every curse of this world off of us, and, like

Jesus, when we come out of the water, we receive the power of the Holy Spirit.

Eating the Matzah

At this point, you pull out—or resurrect—the broken piece of matzah. As the leader eats it, all the participants eat portions of the matzah at their table settings. As you eat it, tell your children about the unleavened bread. First Corinthians says that Jesus is our unleavened Bread:

> *For indeed Christ, our Passover, was sacrificed for us. Therefore let us keep the feast, not with old leaven, nor with the leaven of malice and wickedness, but with the unleavened bread of sincerity and truth.*
> (1 Corinthians 5:7–8)

On that Last Passover Supper, when Jesus picked up the bread and said, "*Take, eat; this is My body*" (Matthew 26:26), He was saying, in effect, "In Me there is no leaven; in Me there is no guile; in Me there are no impurities of any kind. I am the unspotted, unblemished Lamb of God." When He added, "As often as you eat this, do it in remembrance of Me" (see 1 Corinthians 11:24–26), He did so because He knew the disciples were going to be eating this unleavened bread for the next seven days—and for the rest of their lives.

The Maror (Bitter Herbs)

By this point, you may be wondering what to do with that apple, honey, and nut mixture called *charoset*. Well, you're about to find out. Take a pinch of the maror, or bitter herbs (horseradish, the horseradish root shavings, or the romaine lettuce), and put some charoset on it, then brush it off and eat it. Shaking off the charoset symbolizes how hard the Israelites worked in Egypt, combining a food that brings tears to the eyes (the maror, representing slavery) with one that resembles the mortar used to build Egyptian cities and storehouses (the charoset).

When you taste the horseradish, it may bring tears to your eyes. One born-again rabbi says that the herbs not only represent the bitterness of slavery, but they also ensure that we as Christians weep over what Jesus went through for us and never take it for granted. This Lamb of God was willing to be beaten, humiliated, stripped naked, and spat upon. His beard was ripped from His face. The reality of what Jesus suffered should bring tears to our eyes. If it doesn't, perhaps we need a little taste of bitterness to help remind us. Perhaps we need to get on our knees and plead for God to do a new thing in us.

The charoset is actually quite tasty, so feel free to spread some liberally on the matzah bread during and after the meal. When I eat it, I am reminded that I may be *in* this world, but I am no longer *of* this world. I don't care what Wall Street people say; I don't care what medical people say. I'm not trusting in the world anymore. I'm not building my life in the world anymore. I'm working to build God's kingdom as He is building His temple in me. It's not a temple of mortar and bricks, but one of flesh and blood that houses the Holy of Holies inside of us. We're not building bricks and mortar for some pagan temple. We're not serving some god who will get mad at us and forsake us. We're working for the God who loves us more than we will ever understand with a love that surpasses every understanding. Every time I feel tired of working for God, I remember that I used to work for the devil, and it did me no good. Now, I'm working for the King of Kings.

Now, take the other two slices of matzah and place some of the maror between them, making a kind of horseradish sandwich. This is called "the bread of affliction." For the Jews, matzah represents the food they ate in slavery and the manna God provided as they wandered in the desert. It's to remind them that, no matter what affliction they encounter in life, they never want to return to slavery, just as we never want to return to our ways of sin.

> **Never are we to turn back, quit, or return to slavery and sin. God will always bring us miracles.**

In truth, there will be times while serving the Lord when you will find yourself in the desert, when you will need to draw water from a rock, or when you will need God's provision of manna. The answer is always to trust God. Never are we to turn back, quit, or return to slavery and sin. God will always bring us miracles.

The Seder Dinner

In the Jewish tradition, meals are actually blessed afterward. This makes sense, since you would normally thank someone for something after receiving it, not before. I, however, still find it hard not to be thankful on the front end.

> Father, I bless this meal. May there be released a double portion of blessing. Whatever the needs are—physical, financial, family, whatever—may they be met. Father, may that blessing be doubled on our lives tonight, in the name of Jesus, our Messiah. Amen.

The meal begins with the eating of the hard-boiled egg, which represents the holiday offering brought in the days of the temple. The meat of this animal constituted the main part of the Passover meal. Today, the egg is a traditional part of the Seder meal, just as cranberries, stuffing, and turkey are a part of our Thanksgiving feast.

Again, as in the Sabbath meal, there are wide variations as to what you might serve. A rather typical Seder meal would include items such as:

+ roast lamb (although chicken or turkey is okay, too),
+ spinach or another dark green vegetable,
+ a green salad with dressing,
+ a hard-boiled egg,
+ rice, seasoned with herbs,
+ matzah (flat bread), and
+ charoset (dessert).

The Afikomen

In Greek, *afikomen* means "dessert." In ancient times, it was the last morsel of the Passover lamb eaten at the end of the festival meal. Today, it is represented by half of the middle matzah, which, when broken off, is placed back with the others until the end of the meal. For us, this also symbolizes the Messiah, who will come to restore all things.

As the leader eats the matzah, all the participants should eat portions of their matzahs, as well.

The Cup of Redemption

Now, we come to the third cup, which is the cup of redemption. Here, I like to read from 1 Peter 1:18–19:

Knowing that you were not redeemed with corruptible things, like silver or gold, from your aimless conduct received by tradition from your fathers, but with the precious blood of Christ, as of a lamb without blemish and without spot.

We have been redeemed. The word *redeemed* means "to be seen." Through the blood of Jesus, we are re-seen—literally, "seen again" as children of the promises and the covenants of God. We are not just forgiven, but we are also seen in a whole new light. In Leviticus 16, after they sacrificed the lamb, Aaron, the high priest, dipped his finger in the blood of that lamb and went into the Holy of Holies, where he sprinkled it on the mercy seat of the ark of the covenant seven different times. Seven is a very significant number.

Accounting for Every Drop of Blood

Did you know that Jesus did not shed His blood only on the cross? There were actually seven places where Jesus shed His blood. Just as God declared to Israel that they had to collect all of the blood from their sacrificial lamb, so we must account for all of the blood that was shed by the Lamb of God.

1. He bled in the garden of Gethsemane. *"And being in agony, He prayed more earnestly. Then His sweat became like great drops of blood falling down to the ground"* (Luke 22:44). Medical experts agree that intense stress and agony can cause blood vessels just under the skin to burst, causing blood to seep to the surface.

2. He bled at the whipping post. Jesus was not just whipped but also flogged with strips of leather that had pieces of bone or metal at the ends to rip at the flesh.

3. He bled from the crown of thorns. *"When they had twisted a crown of thorns, they put it on His head"* (Matthew 27:29). Biblical scholars believe these thorns were three to four inches long and were pressed into His skull.

4. He bled when His hands were pierced. The nails actually went through a natural hole in the wrist. If the Romans would have put nails through the victim's hands, the bones would have been broken and crushed, and the victim's weight would cause his body to tear away. Nailing the victim through the wrist, however, also caused significant bleeding from the many blood vessels in that area.

5. He bled when His feet were pierced. The cause of death in crucifixion was actually suffocation. The victim's chest cavity would sink, and the only way to get a breath was to push up on the nails in the feet to raise the chest in order to get some air. What excruciating torture! Death was normally hastened by breaking the legs of the victim so he could no longer push up to breathe, resulting in suffocation. But we know that in Jesus' case, this was not necessary, because He gave up His life—nobody took it from Him.

6. He bled when His side was pierced. *"One of the soldiers pierced His side with a spear, and immediately blood and water came out"* (John 19:34).

7. He bled when He was *"wounded for our transgressions, He was bruised for our iniquities"* (Isaiah 53:5). Bruising refers to internal bleeding. Jesus bled internally because His suffering was for your body, soul, and spirit—inside and out.

Just as the Israelites had to collect all of the blood of the Passover lamb, so the cup of redemption must include all of the blood that Jesus shed. Jesus' blood is our authority and anointing. When the angel of death and curse comes to our door, it needs to see the blood that you have applied to the door of your life. Without that blood, the enemy can come into your life, even if you are a child of God. But when we put that blood on the door,

Jesus' blood is our authority and anointing.

making Jesus our once-and-forever Passover Lamb, He is able to break the curses of addiction, sickness, and poverty. Every curse is broken, and every blessing is released.

In Communion, we always distribute the bread and the cup in one quick event. But in Passover, the breaking of the bread and the cup of redemption are separated by the Seder meal. This is just how it happened in Luke:

> Likewise He also took the cup **after supper**, saying, "This cup is the new covenant in My blood, which is shed for you."
>
> (Luke 22:20, emphasis added)

The cup of redemption buys back our prosperity, buys back our victory, buys back our health, buys back our joy, and buys back everything else that we're looking for. That's why, when Jesus hung on the cross, He didn't say, "It's in progress," and He didn't say, "I'm working on it." He said, "It is finished!" (John 19:30). The cup of redemption is to release the power of God's blessing into every area of your life. Let's say a blessing over the third cup:

> Father, we thank You that by the blood of our Lamb, by the blood of Jesus, the Lamb of the world, the Lamb of God, that every curse is broken and every blessing is released. We receive it, in Jesus' name. Amen and amen.

The Cup of Consummation

The fourth cup is the cup of consummation. It's the cup of the final thing. This is the cup that Jesus set down, saying, "I will not drink of the fruit of the vine until the kingdom of God comes" (Luke 22:18). He was telling the disciples that there would come a time when they would be together again at the wedding supper of the Lamb. "I won't drink it until we are together again." When Jesus comes again, He's not coming for a bride who's bruised, busted, and disgusted. He's coming for a beautiful bride without spot and without wrinkle. He's coming for a bride who is seeing the manifestation of the power of God in every single area of life. Jesus said, "When you drink this, remember Me. I told you that I am coming back, and I told you that I am going to release My power. I will do these things through the power of My blood."

So, lift the cup of consummation and realize that Jesus is coming, but He's not coming back for a bunch of losers. When we go to be with Jesus—and I believe He is coming soon—we need to be prepared for the outpouring of God's blessing. As Israel marched out of slavery with all of Egypt's wealth, so we will march out healed, whole, and fully blessed. Lift your cup and say a blessing over it.

> Father, we thank You for the blood. We thank You that Jesus shed His blood to set us free. We thank You that You are going to send Jesus back for us—His glorious bride, manifesting all the joy, goodness, and blessing that come from knowing Jesus Christ as our Passover Lamb. I release that anointing in the name of Yeshua, in the name of Jesus, our Messiah.

Drink from the cup of consummation and say, *"mazel tov,"* which means "good fortune and blessing."

The Cup for Elijah

At the end of the Seder, one final cup is poured for the prophet Elijah. At some Seder meals, there is even an empty place setting for him. Traditionally, Elijah is said to visit each home on Seder night as a foreshadowing of his future arrival at the end of the days, when he will come to announce the arrival of the Jewish Messiah. A child is sent to the door to see if Elijah is there. If not, the door is left open. We do this so the rest of the world can hear the Word of God, because our Father, in His favor, has given us at least one more day to tell the world about the Lamb of God—Jesus Christ, our Savior—before He returns.

Next Year in Jerusalem

Each time a Jewish family celebrates Passover, they end by saying, "Next year in Jerusalem." When they go through Passover, they remember being in bondage and slavery. They remember going through the desert place. They remember being a nation dispersed and persecuted around the world. After being routed from Israel by the Romans around A.D. 70 and having their population dispersed around the globe, Jews for the next two thousand years ended Passover by saying, "Maybe next year we will have a home." Finally, it happened. They have their nation, and they have Jerusalem. Do you realize that next year, we could be celebrating Passover with the Lamb Himself?

God told the Jews to celebrate Passover *"with a belt on your waist, your sandals on your feet, and your staff in your hand"* (Exodus 12:11) as a reminder of how suddenly His deliverance could come. The children of Israel had been slaves in Egypt for centuries. Can you imagine that? God did not bring them out in weeks or months or years, but suddenly. It was so sudden that they didn't have time to bake bread properly. It was so sudden that they had no time to get dressed and pack. They had to be ready to go *now*. Centuries of confinement, bondage, and making someone else's bricks, and God turned it all around in an instant.

Is it any different for us? Jesus could come back at any time, for, as He said, *"Watch therefore, for you do not know what hour your Lord is coming"* (Matthew 24:42). The same could happen for us. I'm not necessarily talking about the rapture. You could receive your physical healing or your financial release. Your marriage could be redeemed, or a family member could be freed from addiction. It can happen in the blink of an eye. Why do you think God told us to remember the Passover? Because there is supernatural power in the Word of God that can change your entire world this very day.

The Feast of Firstfuits

The third feast that takes place during this seven-day period occurs on the second night and is called the Feast of Firstfruits. This was a much more important remembrance in the agricultural climate of biblical times.

Barley was the first crop to be planted in winter. By Passover, it was just beginning to ripen for its spring harvest. By Levitical law, farmers were to cut a sheaf of the crop and, in a carefully prescribed and meticulous ceremony, bring it into the temple and present it to God.

When you come into the land which I give to you, and reap its harvest, then you shall bring a sheaf of the firstfruits of your harvest to the priest. He shall wave the sheaf before the Lord, to be accepted on your behalf; on the day after the Sabbath the priest shall wave it.

(Leviticus 23:10–11)

The Lord's acceptance of the firstfruits was a pledge on His part of a full harvest to come. On the Christian timeline, the Feast of Firstfruits occurs on the evening before Christ's resurrection is celebrated. It has become a symbol of new birth.

Following Jesus' ascension into heaven, major doctrinal debates began to divide the early church. Most notably, some people at the church at Corinth began to spread the false Hellenistic belief called gnosticism, which rejected the concept of a physical resurrection; therefore, it rejected the physical resurrection of Christ. Gnostics recognized only the immortality of the soul.

The apostle Paul weighed in on the subject by suggesting that if there was no bodily resurrection, then Christ was not raised from the dead, their faith was in vain, their loved ones who had died in Christ had perished, and hope was gone. Fortunately, he used the Feast of Firstfuits to dispel this notion.

But now Christ is risen from the dead, and has become the firstfruits of those who have fallen asleep. For since by man came death, by Man also came the resurrection of the dead. For as in Adam all die, even so in Christ all shall be made alive. But each one in his own order: Christ the firstfruits, afterward those who are Christ's at His coming.

(1 Corinthians 15:20–23)

Paul had in mind the first sheaf (firstfruits) of the barley harvest. When God accepted the firstfruits, they became the guarantee that the rest of the crop would, indeed, be harvested. On the day of the Feast of Firstfruits, Jesus Himself became our "firstfruit" offering. Although a number of people mentioned in the Bible were resurrected from the dead (including Jairus' daughter and Lazarus), they eventually died again in due season. Jesus, however, was the first to be resurrected from death and the grave, never to die again. By that action, God guaranteed that the rest of the crop, those He calls His children, would one day join the harvest.

The Feast of Passover, together with the Feasts of Unleavened Bread and Firstfruits, is an opportunity to tell our children, and be reminded ourselves, that Passover is not just an empty religious observance. Rather, it is to remind us that the coming harvest has been guaranteed and that we may be called to the New Jerusalem at any moment. Therefore, we'd better be ready to go and take as many with us as we possibly can.

God knows that we need these reminders. He knows that we can get so caught up in this life that we forget that our lives are but the blink of an eye compared to eternity. This life is only to prepare us for the next life. Are you ready to go?

10

The Feast of Pentecost

The former account I made, O Theophilus, of all that Jesus began both to do and teach, until the day in which He was taken up, after He through the Holy Spirit had given commandments to the apostles whom He had chosen, to whom He also presented Himself alive after His suffering by many infallible proofs, being seen by them during forty days and speaking of the things pertaining to the kingdom of God. And being assembled together with them, He commanded them not to depart from Jerusalem, but to wait for the Promise of the Father, "which," He said, "you have heard from Me; for John truly baptized with water, but you shall be baptized with the Holy Spirit not many days from now." Therefore, when they had come together, they asked Him, saying, "Lord, will You at this time restore the kingdom to Israel?" And He said to them, "It is not for you to know times or seasons which the Father has put in His own authority. But you shall receive power when the Holy Spirit has come upon you; and you shall be witnesses to Me in Jerusalem, and in all Judea and Samaria, and to the end of the earth." (Acts 1:1–8)

The last thing that Jesus did on this earth was instruct His followers to wait for the coming of the Holy Spirit. I want you to realize why this is so important. If you're leaving your children or spouse or loved ones and you're never going to see them or speak to them again face-to-face, the last thing you say to them is probably going to be something important. It won't be some trivial piece of information. In His last words, Jesus commanded His followers not to leave Jerusalem until they had received the Holy Spirit.

> **Our traditions can limit the work of the Holy Spirit.**

Why is this so important? We who call ourselves "Spirit-filled Christians" can often miss the power behind the Holy Spirit. Just as our traditions can make the Word of God *of no effect* (Mark 7:13), I believe our traditions can also limit the work of the Holy Spirit. Jesus wasn't commanding His followers to remain in Jerusalem until they had learned to fall down and laugh. He wasn't commanding them to stay until they had learned how to perform a "courtesy flop" to the ground when somebody prayed for them. Don't get me wrong. I'm not saying that stuff is not of God, but there is more to the Holy Spirit than just laughing or falling over backward. I like what my friend Creflo Dollar said: "I don't mind you falling down, but when you get back up, something ought to have changed. Something ought to have happened!" Jesus was commanding them to stay put, because in a few days, they were going to receive the Holy Spirit in power and might!

> *When the Day of Pentecost had fully come, they were all with one accord in one place. And suddenly there came a sound from heaven, as of a rushing mighty wind, and it filled the whole house where they were sitting. Then there appeared to them divided tongues, as of fire, and one sat upon each of them. And they were all filled with the Holy Spirit and began to speak with other tongues, as the Spirit gave them utterance.*
>
> (Acts 2:1–4)

Once again, we can miss what is going on here if we read Scripture as Christians and not as first-century Jews. We may think Pentecost happened on the day that the Holy Spirit fell, but it's actually just the opposite—the Holy Spirit fell on the day of Pentecost!

Jesus was about to ascend into heaven. Just before He went, however, He commanded His followers not to go anywhere until they had received the Holy Spirit. A few days later, when they were all gathered for the Jewish feast of Pentecost, or *Shavuot*, the Holy Spirit fell on them. The Bible says that when it came, there was thunder and lightning and tongues of fire, and they all began to speak in other tongues.

> *Parthians and Medes and Elamites, those dwelling in Mesopotamia, Judea and Cappadocia, Pontus and Asia, Phrygia and Pamphylia, Egypt and the parts of Libya adjoining Cyrene, visitors from Rome, both Jews and proselytes, Cretans and Arabs; we hear them speaking in our own tongues the wonderful works of God.* (Acts 2:9–11)

Whatever languages were in existence at that time, they began to speak them. It was a miracle of God. They were praising Him in tongues they didn't know. The people around them who had gathered for Pentecost were from other countries and heard their own home tongues begin spoken in praise and worship. They knew it had to be supernatural, and a great revival took place.

I used to live in Arizona, and I can remember my pastor sharing a story like this. One day, as a young man—before he was a pastor—he was in a prayer room before church, speaking in tongues and praying to God. All of a sudden, he spoke in a tongue he had never experienced before. When he came into the service, he could feel the Spirit of God moving. Suddenly, he stood up and started speaking in this new tongue, while across the auditorium a woman began to interpret. Interpreting is a gift sorely needed in the church today. This is what happens when you don't understand the tongues being spoken, but God gives you their meaning to share with the congregation.

As this went on, two Navajo women burst into tears, ran down to the front, and fell on their faces, repenting before God. Apparently, the man who would later become my pastor was speaking fluent Navajo as the woman interpreted, word for word. Both of them were Caucasian, without a drop of Native American blood. Navajo is one of the hardest languages in the world to learn, but he spoke it fluently by the Spirit of God, and the woman interpreted it by the same Spirit. These two women, however, needed no interpretation. They instantly recognized their native tongue being spoken in church. God was essentially saying to these Navajo women, "I know who you are, and I'm reaching out to you. Receive My love. Return to Me." In response, they received the Lord as their Savior that day. Those are true gifts of the Spirit.

The Day of Pentecost

To understand what the day of Pentecost truly is, we must go back to the book of Exodus.

> *It came to pass on the third day, in the morning, that there were thunderings and lightnings, and a thick cloud on the mountain; and the sound of the trumpet was very loud, so that all the people who were in the camp trembled. And Moses brought the people out of the camp to meet with God, and they stood at the foot of the mountain. Now Mount Sinai was completely in smoke, because the Lord descended upon it in fire. Its smoke ascended like the smoke of a furnace, and the whole mountain quaked greatly.* (Exodus 19:16–18)

In Hebrew, this is *Shavuot,* or Pentecost. It is the day when God gave the world the beginnings of what would be the Bible. Four thousand years later, when Jesus commanded His disciples not to leave, He then gave us the Holy Spirit so that we could better understand the Bible and walk in the power we have through the resurrection and the blood of Jesus Christ.

> **The power of the Holy Spirit is not ours to put on a show; it's to bring down fire from heaven.**

When the Holy Spirit fell, the Bible says the place was shaking, and there was thunder and lightning and tongues of fire. Four thousand years earlier, on Mount Sinai, when Moses received the Word of God, there was also shaking and thunder and lightning and fire. The power of the Holy Spirit is to give us fire—the anointing, wisdom, and authority that Jesus paid for when His blood was spilled. We need this power, because Jesus said, "Wherever you go, tell them the kingdom of heaven is at hand, then heal the sick, raise the dead, and cast out demons." (See Mark 16:15–18). The power of the Holy Spirit is not ours to put on a show; it's to bring down fire from heaven—the power that Jesus paid for.

A Double Blessing of Harvest

> *You shall count for yourselves from the day after the Sabbath, from the day that you brought the sheaf of the wave offering: seven Sabbaths shall*

be completed. Count fifty days to the day after the seventh Sabbath; then you shall offer a new grain offering to the LORD. You shall bring from your dwellings two wave loaves of two-tenths of an ephah. They shall be of fine flour; they shall be baked with leaven. They are the first-fruits to the LORD. (Leviticus 23:15–17)

The word *sheaf* is translated from the Hebrew word *omer*, meaning "a measure." All of the farmers in Israel were to bring a sheaf of barley in the Passover season to present to God. This was the Feast of Firstfruits. It was an offering to ensure the maturing of their harvest. God told them to count seven Sabbaths and one day—fifty days—from that day.

Fifty is the number of Pentecost. There were fifty days from Egypt to Mount Sinai, where Moses received the Word of God. Fifty days is also the number of Jubilee, when God cancels all your debts, sets everybody free, and brings the new harvest that we've been waiting for. Jubilee is the day when God restores all the blessings we have lost, rejected, or missed out on.

Fifty Days of Preparation

The Talmud is a collection of writings by Jewish rabbis and scholars commentating on Jewish law, life, and customs. In the Talmud, many Jewish rabbis wonder why God waited fifty days to give Israel His Word. Rabbis teach that our redemption is not complete when we are merely set free. Redemption is complete only when you receive the Word of God and fulfill it. Many Christians come out of the slavery of "Egypt," but they don't receive God's Word and live by it. As a result, they find themselves wandering in the desert.

Some Talmud teachings claim that after four hundred years of captivity in Egypt, Israel had become so worldly that God couldn't speak to them. Even though they were the children of God, they were still acting just like the world. Look at the church today. Is it much different? Here's a thought: if we're born again, we probably should not be fornicating anymore. Here's another thought: if we're Christians, we probably should not be stealing from the workplace. If we're Christians, we should look different from the world. We shouldn't have to tell people we're Christians. People should be able to see that simply by observing what we do and what we don't do.

Therefore, God created a countdown, a time of preparation and anticipation for receiving His Word. It is a time for us to make sure we are ready for His revelation by double-checking our characters. *Am I serving God with all my heart? Is He number one in my life, or has He been replaced by some kind of idol in my life? Am I treating my neighbor right? Am I gossiping or backbiting? Am I unforgiving? I want God to forgive me, but maybe I'm not forgiving others.* God said, "You need to make sure your character is lined up so that on this day, fifty days from now, I can bring you a double portion of your coming harvest."

Celebrating the Feast of Pentecost

> God wants to release biblical revelation.

God wants to release Pentecost on us. God wants to release Shavuot. He wants to release biblical revelation. God delivered His people out of the bondages of slavery and death in Egypt, and then, fifty days later, He gave them the Torah, a path to walk on. Thirty-five hundred years later, God delivered His people out of the slavery of sin and death, and then, fifty days later, He gave them the Holy Spirit, a guide to keep them on the path. He said, "Wherever you go, I'm going with you. I'm giving you all authority. Go into all the world, and I will confirm My Word with signs, wonders, and miracles." The fifty days after Passover—the counting of the omer—is the preparation for the Word of God and for a revelation of His Spirit.

How do we keep Pentecost? First, it is a time of double blessing. Each Pentecost Sabbath, we anoint everybody's hands for prosperity. We lay hands on every forehead for the wisdom and the anointing and the power and the gifts of the Spirit—of the Holy Spirit. Second, it's a time of Jubilee, so we pray for all curses to be broken and all debts to be cancelled, in Jesus' name. Third, it's a Sabbath of Sabbaths—seven weeks of the seventh day. It is to receive an extra measure of joy and peace and to release a double anointing on your children and your children's children.

A Sabbath of Sabbaths—it's a double blessing.

11

The Feast of Rosh Hashanah (New Year)

Rosh Hashanah literally means "head of the year," and it is commonly referred to as the "Jewish New Year." It is celebrated in the fall, usually near the end of September, and it begins a ten-day period of repentence that concludes with Yom Kippur, the Day of Atonement. In Hebrew, Rosh Hashanah also means "the opening of the gate." It is the opening of heaven's gates. Just as we often reflect and self-evaluate on New Year's Day, January 1, we also judge ourselves on Rosh Hashanah. Am I paying my tithe? Am I sacrificing? Am I being kind? Am I forgiving? Am I gracious? Am I loving? These are not requirements for salvation, but they are ways of fulfilling the two commandments that Jesus said fulfilled all the law and the prophets: love God and love others. If we are walking with Christ in this, the gates of the kingdom are opened for us with all the blessings of heaven. Then, the glorious church of Jesus Christ will be without spot or wrinkle.

The right hand of the LORD is exalted; the right hand of the LORD does valiantly. I shall not die, but live, and declare the works of the LORD. The LORD has chastened me severely, but He has not given me over to death. (Psalm 118:16–18)

In the next year,

+ I will live and not die.

+ I won't go broke.

+ I won't get sick.

+ My marriage won't die.

+ I am going to live and declare the works of the Lord.

"The LORD has chastened me severely." What does that mean? In Israel, during every day in the thirty days leading to Rosh Hashanah, the rabbi would blow an ancient trumpet—the *shofar.* The shofar was a warning that Rosh Hashanah was coming. During those thirty days, God would speak to the people. "You have been gossiping; you have been backbiting; you have been cheating God; you have not been forgiving." For thirty days, the Lord would chasten them. They knew that *"as a man chastens his son, so the LORD your God chastens you"* (Deuteronomy 8:5). Today, we know that *"whom the LORD loves He chastens"* (Hebrews 12:6). The people were aware that if they had not forgiven others, the next year would not be good. If they had been gossiping and hurtful, the next year would not be good.

The good news was, *"He has not given me over to death."* In other words, we may have been doing some bad things, but God has not given up on us. He is blowing that trumpet to remind us that a new year—a new beginning—is on the way. Old things pass away; all things are becoming new. (See 2 Corinthians 5:17.) Now, look at these verses of Psalm 118:

> *Open to me the gates of righteousness; I will go through them, and I will praise the LORD. This is the gate of the LORD, through which the righteous shall enter.* (verses 19–20)

> **We are the righteousness of God. We are God's acts of charity by grace.**

Remember that the word *righteousness* is the Hebrew word *tsedkah,* meaning "charity." We are saved because of God's charity. He looked at us and sent Jesus to be our Messiah—to die so that we might live. We are the righteousness of God. We are God's acts of charity by grace.

Let's look at the names associated with Rosh Hashanah. *Rosh* means "new" and *Hashanah* means "year," so this is the new year. On God's calendar, there are two new years. Passover is the spiritual new year when you and I were born. It is the day when Jesus died on the cross. The Last

Supper, in which Jesus led his followers in what we now call Communion, was actually a celebration of Passover. He broke the bread (His body) and drank the cup (His blood) in order to say, in effect, "I am the Passover Lamb." Passover, therefore, is the *spiritual* new year.

Rosh Hashanah is the *physical* or *civil* new year. It is similar to how some Christians celebrate their physical birthdays, the days they were born, and their spiritual birthdays, the days they were born again. Rosh Hashanah is the beginning of God's civil calendar, when He wipes away the last year through Jesus Christ. The only way we can share in this is if we have Jesus so that we have been *"grafted in"* (Romans 11:17) with these covenant promises. If you have Jesus, the Abrahamic covenants are also our covenants.

The Feast of Trumpets

According to the Talmud—a record of rabbinic discussions pertaining to Jewish law, ethics, customs, and history—God opens up three books of judgment on Rosh Hashanah. The first, the Book of the Righteous, has all the names of those who have returned to God. The second, the Book of the Wholly Wicked, has all the names of the unrighteous written in it. The third book has the names of all the intermediates—those who have not yet been judged and have ten days to repent. If they repent by the Day of Atonement, Yom Kippur, their names are then added to the Book of the Righteousness. Does this sound familiar? Remember the words of Jesus:

> I know your works, that you are neither cold nor hot. I could wish you were cold or hot. So then, because you are lukewarm, and neither cold nor hot, I will vomit you out of My mouth.   (Revelation 3:15–16)

The lukewarm ones are those who know the Messiah but are not doing anything with that knowledge. The lukewarm person pleads, "Lord, may my name be put in the Book of the Righteous."

If you are a Christian as old as I am, perhaps you've seen movies like *A Thief in the Night* or *Image of the Beast* in which the rapture comes, and a preacher is not taken. A similar situation occurs in the fiction series *Left Behind*. The preachers in these stories were lukewarm. Know this: God does not want to leave *anybody* behind! That is why He blows the trumpets and sends us prophets, a Messiah, and the Holy Spirit, all saying the same thing: "Get right; get right; get right." We are not just talking about sin; we are talking about knowing the truth but not serving the Lord. On Rosh Hashanah, according to the Talmud, God opens up three books and shows them to our spirits. We reflect on our lives. Are we serving God? Are we doing anything for the kingdom? Are we being salt and light in the world? We should want to be doing these things, not only so we can make heaven our home, but also so we might experience heaven down here on earth and receive God's blessing over the next year.

> **On Rosh Hashanah, God is waking us up so He can give us a wonderful new year.**

Remember, the word *righteous* means being salt and light in the world. Instead of being part of the world's problem, we need to be part of the world's solution. On Rosh Hashanah, God is waking us up so He can give us a wonderful new year. This is why it is sometimes called the "Feast of Trumpets." God is saying, "Wake up. Get ready. You have ten days to reflect and get your life together."

Then the LORD spoke to Moses, saying, "Speak to the children of Israel, saying: 'In the seventh month, on the first day of the month, you shall have a sabbath-rest, a memorial of blowing of trumpets, a holy convocation. You shall do no customary work on it; and you shall offer an offering made by fire to the LORD.'" (Leviticus 23:23–25)

There are three reasons in the Bible to blow the shofar. The first is to announce a new king. When Jesus comes back for us, the trumpet will blow, and He will return with a shout. For thirty days before Rosh Hashanah, rabbis blow the shofar reminding the people to get ready. When Jesus returns, He will come not as a Lamb but as a King to set up the new Jerusalem. Why should we be blowing the trumpet? What if He comes tomorrow and you are lukewarm? The blowing of the trumpet announces the coming of the King.

Second, it is to call the army of the Lord to battle. David's troubles with Bathsheba occurred because he stayed away from the battle. If we are to be ready for the rapture, we need to be in the battle. Don't be caught at home when the battle rages. What will keep you entering into battle instead of becoming lukewarm and slinking away?

Third, the blowing of the shofar is a call to worship. It calls the lukewarm back into worship.

Therefore He says: "Awake, you who sleep, arise from the dead, and Christ will give you light." See then that you walk circumspectly, not as fools but as wise, redeeming the time, because the days are evil.
(Ephesians 5:14–16)

Here, the apostle Paul quoted the book of Isaiah and said, "Wake up! Hear the sound of the trumpet. Let it awaken you out of your sleep, because if you are asleep, you are not redeeming the time. The King is coming; the Bridegroom is coming; wake up, because when He comes and finds you asleep, and you say, 'Lord, don't forget me,' it will be too late."

Parable of the Ten Virgins

In the parable of the ten virgins, the women were virgins because they received the Messiah, and their sins were washed clean as snow. Five of the virgins, however, were foolish and had no oil in their lamps to be lights in the world.

And at midnight a cry was heard: "Behold, the bridegroom is coming; go out to meet him!" Then all those virgins arose and trimmed their lamps. And the foolish said to the wise, "Give us some of your oil, for our lamps are going out." But the wise answered, saying, "No, lest there should not be enough for us and you; but go rather to those who sell, and buy for yourselves." And while they went to buy, the bridegroom came, and those who were ready went in with him to the wedding; and the door was shut. Afterward the other virgins came also, saying, "Lord, Lord, open to us!" But he answered and said, "Assuredly, I say to you, I do not know you." (Matthew 25:6–12)

Five virgins had their lamps full of oil, but five were left behind. How many are going to be left behind?

For the Lord Himself will descend from heaven with a shout, with the voice of an archangel, and with the trumpet of God. And the dead in Christ will rise first. Then we who are alive and remain shall be caught up together with them in the clouds to meet the Lord in the air. And thus we shall always be with the Lord. Therefore comfort one another with these words. (1 Thessalonians 4:16–18)

If the Lord comes back tonight, we are going to hear the shout and the blast, but we will hear them *before* He comes. Why before He comes? Because He does not want to leave anyone behind. He wants everyone to make it, so He is going to blow that trumpet, saying, "Get ready!" When a woman gives birth, it does not happen without labor pains coming first. There are signs and tremblings warning of what is to come. God is stirring things up. He is moving so that you know when it is time. When the time of a child's birth comes near, the wise husband will have his overnight bag packed, his car full of gasoline, and proper directions to the hospital. Woe to the expectant father who is not prepared when the moment arrives!

The same thing holds true for believers on earth. When the rapture takes place, we had better be found serving God. Are you ready? Is there something you need to do to prepare? Do you need to forgive? Do you need to change things in your life? Wake up! In the same way that you don't want to miss out on the Lord's second coming, you also don't want to miss His blessings for your life over the next year.

Let me ask you something. Has your fire gone out? Have you become lukewarm? Over the years, the winds blow, and the bride must keep relighting that fire. Keep relighting that candle so that when the Bridegroom returns, He can see your candle as a sign that you are ready to go. If your fire has gone out, Rosh Hashanah is your night to rededicate yourself to the Bridegroom and to prepare for a year of blessing like you have never seen before.

You've probably heard that Jesus is coming *"as a thief in the night"* (2 Peter 3:10). But do you understand that He is coming as a thief in the night only for those who are not looking for Him? He is not going to surprise those who are waiting obediently—those who recognize the signs. I believe we are already experiencing some of those signs. We are seeing wars and rumors of wars. We are seeing Israel surrounded by enemies. We are seeing governments besieged by terrorism talking about putting identification chips into citizens. Bible prophecy talks about the end times and the formation of a one-world government. Recently, China proposed the use of a common world currency. I am telling you, the birth pangs are here. The Messiah is not going to catch us unaware, but if He does not come this year, let us prepare for His blessings. Let us prepare for Him to shift the wealth of the wicked into our hands. Let us become the bride adorned with all the anointing and the power of God.

Remember when the disciples came to Jesus and asked, "Lord, when are You coming back?" Jesus' answer was, "I don't know." *"Of that day and hour no one knows, not even the angels in heaven, nor the Son, but only the Father"* (Mark 13:32). He was not putting them off. He really doesn't know. You might say, "I thought Jesus knew everything." He knows everything but that. God alone knows the exact time. In the meantime, Jesus is keeping busy.

When you go to the Middle East, you will see houses that look a little odd. You'll see the main house, which has been there for many years; then, there will be another section of the house that looks as though it has been there for ten years. Another, newer section looks like it may be only five years old. Then, there will be yet another section that is still being built. This is part of a long-standing Jewish tradition.

A father may have a son who has become engaged to a woman in their village or another village. A typical engagement lasts at least a year. During that time, the couple is completely separated. The groom remains at his father's house preparing a "mansion"—one of those funky additions. The bride, meanwhile, is to be bringing honor to the family by remaining a virtuous woman. During this separation, the groom's father may send spies to observe the woman. If she changes over that year, the father will not let the son come back for the bride. We are not the bride of Christ yet. We are engaged to Him. When the rapture comes, and we sit at the wedding supper of the Lamb, then we will become the bride. Until then, the Father is watching us. Rosh Hashanah is that time when the Father says, "Get ready."

The Day of Turning

Therefore, Rosh Hashanah is, first, a new year—a reflection and a new beginning. Second, it is the Feast of Trumpets—calling us to be ready.

> **This year can be a turning point for God's miracle in your life.**

Third, it is a time of repentance, or turning. You and I are making the decision to turn back to the Father. If you do not know the Father, turn to Him. If you are a prodigal son, a child of God who has slipped away, turn back to the Father. If you are lukewarm, turn back to the fire. If you are already on fire, stay on fire. As we turn toward God, He will turn our world around. This year can be a turning point for God's miracle in your life.

If any of you lacks wisdom, let him ask of God, who gives to all liberally and without reproach, and it will be given to him. (James 1:5)

James was referring to those who don't see the promises of God. "If you lack wisdom," he said, "why not just ask for it? God will give it." Let's be honest, should all of us be healed? Yes. Should all of us prosper? Yes. If He will save *one* of us, He will save *all* of us. If He will heal *one* of us, He will heal *all* of us. If He will bless *one* of us, He will bless *all* of us. We just need to get turned around. James said if anything is wrong, if there's anything you lack, ask God.

Rosh Hashanah is the night we judge ourselves and turn. The blast of the trumpet is to wake us up. Remember Paul's teaching regarding Communion.

But let a man examine himself, and so let him eat of the bread and drink of the cup. For he who eats and drinks in an unworthy manner eats and drinks judgment to himself, not discerning the Lord's body. For this reason many are weak and sick among you, and many sleep.
(1 Corinthians 11:28–30)

We judge, or examine, ourselves on Rosh Hashanah so that in ten days we will be judged righteous. When Paul said that *"many sleep,"* he did not necessarily mean they are physically dead. When you receive Jesus, you are born again, and heaven is your home, but you can still be dead, or asleep, to the promises of God. If you are living in sin, you are asleep and in need of resurrection. Some are asleep to being righteous and doing good works for others. For them, the promises of God are dead. Righteous does not only mean that we have received Jesus as our Savior. That is step one, but now that we have received Jesus as our Lord and Savior, we need to become salt and light to the world. What if you woke up this morning and said, "Whom can I bless? Whom can I be an encouragement to? Whom can I bring joy to? Whom can I remind that the kingdom of God is at hand?

If you are not bringing acts of charity—tzedakah—into the world, you are not righteous. Are you filling your Sabbath tzedakah boxes as a mitzvah for others? Remember, we have only two commandments—love God, and love others as yourselves. Remember Jesus' incredible story of the sheep and the goats? The King condemned the goats, not because of what they did or didn't believe, but because of what they did or didn't do.

> *Then He will also say to those on the left hand, "Depart from Me, you cursed, into the everlasting fire prepared for the devil and his angels: for I was hungry and you gave Me no food; I was thirsty and you gave Me no drink; I was a stranger and you did not take Me in, naked and you did not clothe Me, sick and in prison and you did not visit Me." Then they also will answer Him, saying, "Lord, when did we see You hungry or thirsty or a stranger or naked or sick or in prison, and did not minister to You?" Then He will answer them, saying, "Assuredly, I say to you, inasmuch as you did not do it to one of the least of these, you did not do it to Me." And these will go away into everlasting punishment, but the righteous into eternal life.* (Matthew 25:41–46)

If you want your next year to be blessed, bring all your tithes into the house. Even the widow brought her mite to the tzedakah box—the charity box. She had to be a blessing so that when the trumpet sounded, she would be found to be a giver of kindness. During the next year, she would not need that mite because God would provide her with all she needed and more.

Righteousness is not simply the absence of sin—righteousness is also about doing what is right. Is there someone you need to forgive? Forgive him so God can forgive you. Are you negative? Stop it. You are cursing yourself and blocking your blessing.

> **Righteousness is not simply the absence of sin—righteousness is also about doing what is right.**

It is so easy to be blessed. Each day, you simply get up and say, "God, bless me today." He'll do it. There's nothing wrong with that. But do you know how to bless others who are hungry or thirsty for an act of charity? Each day, you get up and say, "God, give me someone I can bless." Don't forsake the tithe in your local church. Every time you meet with God, you should bring an offering. That is how they did it in the temple. Every time they met, an offering was given. Everyone put something in the tzedakah box, and even the poor widow can make a difference.

But giving is not a magic formula. If you are giving but not treating your wife right, God will not listen to your prayers. So many people give but then kill the seed by being negative, destructive, or selfish. That is why it's not just giving. God says you need to check yourself. You have a new year and ten days to do an inventory, because He wants to bless you this coming year.

12

The Feast of Yom Kippur (Day of Atonement)

Each fall, Jews around the world recognize Yom Kippur, or the Day of Atonement, on the tenth day after Rosh Hashanah. On this night, sundown begins the twenty-four hours of the Feast of Yom Kippur—an appointed time at which God has decided to meet with us in a way that is different from any other time of the year. During this meeting, God writes your name in the Book of Blessing for the next year so that the windows of heaven can be opened over your life, your family, your finances, and your future—windows that cannot be closed for the entire year.

In Jewish synagogues, for the forty days leading up to this night, the people have heard the blowing of the shofar, an ancient trumpet calling for the people of God to wake up. Are we serving God? Are we living for God? Are we being the people God has called us to be as the light of the world and the salt of the earth?

Forty is one of the most significant numbers in the Bible. For forty days and nights, it rained when Noah was on the ark. Moses fasted for forty days to intercede for the children of Israel on Mount Sinai. The twelve spies were sent into Canaan for forty days. Goliath stood and challenged the children of Israel for forty days before David slew him with a stone. For forty days, Jonah warned Ninevah of an oncoming judgment. Jesus was tempted in the wilderness for forty days. Finally, there were forty days between Jesus' resurrection and His ascension into heaven. It represents a time of trial and chastisement—not judgment but more a time of preparation and proving.

187

> **Our God is not a God who desires to punish; He is a God who desires to provide blessings.**

The God we serve is not watching us and waiting for us to make a mistake so He can judge us. He is not eagerly anticipating our failures. On the contrary, He is constantly urging us, "Get right. Get right. Get right!" Why? Because Goliath is going down. The Canaanite may be big, but our God is bigger; Satan may think he has won, but the power of the resurrection is coming. Our God is not a God who desires to punish; He is a God who desires to provide blessings.

We find the basis for Yom Kippur in the book of Leviticus:

Thus Aaron shall come into the Holy Place: with the blood of a young bull as a sin offering, and of a ram as a burnt offering. He shall put the holy linen tunic and the linen trousers on his body; he shall be girded with a linen sash, and with the linen turban he shall be attired. These are holy garments. Therefore he shall wash his body in water, and put them on. (Leviticus 16:3–4)

Before the high priest could enter the Holy of Holies to intervene for the people of God, he first had to make sure he was clean. As Christian leaders and pastors, we can take something from this. Of course, we are saved by grace and not by works, but we need to realize that the shepherds of God's people need to be clean. We need to cleanse the pulpit of drug and alcohol addiction, adultery, and pornography, as well as greed and financial malfeasance. The men and women of God need to live transparent lives. At this point, I am preaching to myself as much as to anyone reading this book.

Aaron shall offer the bull as a sin offering, which is for himself, and make atonement for himself and for his house. He shall take the two goats and present them before the LORD at the door of the tabernacle of meeting. Then Aaron shall cast lots for the two goats: one lot for the LORD and the other lot for the scapegoat. And Aaron shall bring the goat on which the Lord's lot fell, and offer it as a sin offering. But the goat on which the lot fell to be the scapegoat shall be presented alive before the LORD, *to make atonement upon it, and to let it go as the scapegoat into the wilderness.* (Leviticus 16:6–10)

This is Yom Kippur.

Then he shall kill the goat of the sin offering, which is for the people, bring its blood inside the veil, do with that blood as he did with the blood of the bull, and sprinkle it on the mercy seat and before the mercy seat. So he shall make atonement for the Holy Place, because of the uncleanness of the children of Israel, and because of their transgressions, for all their sins; and so he shall do for the tabernacle of meeting which remains among them in the midst of their uncleanness. There shall be no man in the tabernacle of meeting when he goes in to make atonement in the Holy Place, until he comes out, that he may make atonement for himself, for his household, and for all the assembly of Israel. And he shall go out to the altar that is before the LORD, *and make atonement for it, and shall take some of the blood of the bull and some of the blood of the goat, and put it on the horns of the altar all around. Then he shall sprinkle some of the blood on it with his finger seven times, cleanse it, and consecrate it from the uncleanness of the children of Israel. And when he has made an end of atoning for the Holy Place, the tabernacle of meeting, and the altar, he shall bring the live goat.* (verses 15–20)

Remember, there are two offerings.

Aaron shall lay both his hands on the head of the live goat, confess over it all the iniquities of the children of Israel, and all their transgressions, concerning all their sins. (verse 21)

Aaron confessed their sins, but he also confessed the curses, or iniquities, that were on them because of those sins. If someone had stolen something, that was a sin, but the curse on that person's finances, businesses, crops, and herds as a result of the sin was just as bad. That was the *iniquity*. God was not just forgiving his sin, He was also breaking the curse. The God we serve is our Father, and it is His good pleasure to rid us of all of our religious "stinkin' thinkin.'"

On Sundays before church, I am usually upstairs in my church office, huddled with all our pastors. Some of them are praying as I work furiously on finishing the notes for my sermon. Occasionally, I will hear a little voice: "Sabba?" In will come my two grandsons, Asher and Judah. I am telling you, everything stops for those babies. Nothing I had been concerned with can match my love for those two little ones. If I, a flawed and sinful man, can love them so much, how much more do you think a perfect God is able to love us?

When we pray, when we come before God today and say, "Abba Father, I have a need," He stops making universes; He stops listening to the heavenly host; He stops everything and says, "Quiet! My babies are here!" Yes, He is God. Yes, He is omnipotent. Yes, He is omnipresent. More importantly, He is your Dad. When Jesus faced His final crisis in the garden of Gethsemane, He prayed, *"Abba, Father, all things are possible for You"* (Mark 14:36). Jesus was saying, essentially, "Daddy, Father...."

Rabbis teach that God's love is so great that He hears us every day of the year, but on Yom Kippur, He is closer to earth. He is setting up His kingdom, where there will be no more tears; there will be no more sorrow. There will be no lack or pain. On this day, He is closer to setting up His kingdom than on any other day of the year. The Lord is our God every day of the week, but on the Sabbath, everything multiplies. On Yom Kippur, everything multiplies again.

Atonement

Animal sacrifices were abandoned by the Jews after the destruction of their temple, around A.D. 70. While it existed, however, these sacrifices were the primary way in which the Jews worshipped and honored God. First, according to Jewish tradition, we need to realize that two sacrifices were required by God for Israel's atonement—or forgiveness. This was also part of Israel's calendar new year, thus it was the time when God would erase all the sins of the past year. If you are a businessperson, this would be much like a fiscal new year when the books of the past are balanced and closed, and a new book is started.

The priest was in the temple, where he was preparing. He would put on fine, white linen—the only time of the year he wore it. As he was preparing, his helpers came to the door of the temple, bringing with them not one sacrifice but two—according to Scripture, two goats. (See Leviticus 16:7.) He then cast lots to determine which goat would become the sacrifice. This sacrificial animal was then led into the temple, while the other one was left outside. In the outer courts of the temple, the priests placed the sacrifice onto the brazen altar as the high priest cut its throat. The blood of that goat was to cover the sins of Israel. As this sacrifice took place, the priest's white robe became saturated with the animal's blood. In Jewish culture, when something was bloodstained, it became impure and untouchable.

Before the high priest entered the Holy of Holies with the blood of the sacrifice, he removed the soiled robe and hung it in plain view of all the people. Instead of washing only his hands or feet, the other priests completely washed the high priest from head to toe to make sure that there was not one spot of blood remaining on his body. Then, before he appeared before the people again, the high priest put on a new, white robe. His stain-free reappearance was a reminder that no matter what they did, they had come before the Lord, and His mercy was fresh every morning.

From there, the high priest, now washed and clothed in white—a symbol of purity—once again ascended to the altar of God. Because he was now "pure" and about to go into the Holy of Holies to make intercession, no one was allowed to touch him lest he would become defiled. He would chant these words over and over: "Do not touch me with anything of this world, for I have not yet been with the Father." He entered into the Holy of Holies—the only day of the year this was allowed by God—and sprinkled the blood on the mercy seat of the Ark of the Covenant seven times. This was the atonement that released the blessing and forgiveness of God.

> **Our Sacrifice, Jesus, shed His blood and died in plain sight as our permanent atonement for sin.**

Similarly, the moment Jesus died on the cross our sins were washed away, once and for all. I don't care what you did yesterday. I don't care what you did twenty years ago. The devil may try to bring it back up, but Jesus has already washed us clean, and our sins went down the drain. Not one spot of guilt remains. Our Sacrifice, Jesus, shed His blood and died in plain sight as our permanent atonement for sin. This is the basis for the prophecy that says,

> "Come now, and let us reason together," says the LORD, "though your sins are like scarlet, they shall be as white as snow; though they are red like crimson, they shall be as wool." (Isaiah 1:18)

Christians who confess, repent, and plead the blood of Jesus are then forgiven. Through His blood, we are cleansed, though our sins *are red like crimson, they shall be as wool.* There is no condemnation for those who are in Christ Jesus. (See Romans 8:1.) There is no condemnation if we repent. We have to repent. You can't be a born-again drug user. You can't be a born-again fornicator. You have to repent. You have to turn back to God and away from your sinful ways. The moment you do that, His mercy is fresh every morning.

Now, let's go to the book of Hebrews.

> Christ came as High Priest of the good things to come, with the greater and more perfect tabernacle not made with hands, that is, not of this creation. Not with the blood of goats and calves, but with His own blood He entered the Most Holy Place once for all, having obtained eternal redemption. For if the blood of bulls and goats and the ashes of a heifer, sprinkling the unclean, sanctifies for the purifying of the flesh, how much more shall the blood of Christ, who through the eternal Spirit offered Himself without spot to God, cleanse your conscience from dead works to serve the living God? (Hebrews 9:11–14)

Jesus, our High Priest, spotted with blood—the representation of sin—was laid in the grave. When He appeared again and walked out of that tomb, He was *"white as snow"* (Isaiah 1:18). We have been saved from that curse and brought into the resurrected power of our living, loving God, and because of our High Priest who went before us, we are able to stand before God without wrinkle or stain.

> This is the covenant that I will make with them after those days, says the LORD: I will put My laws into their hearts, and in their minds I will write them. (Hebrews 10:16)

Jesus said, "I did not come to do away with the law, but I came to fulfill it." (See Matthew 5:17.) God says, "*I will put My laws into their hearts.*" This is the reason the New Testament is not a *different* covenant but a *better* one. The first Ten Commandments were written on stone; the second Ten Commandments are written on our hearts. Man can break stone, but he cannot break what God has written on the heart. "*'I will put My laws into their hearts, and in their minds I will write them,' then He adds, 'their sins and their lawless deeds I will remember no more'*" (Hebrews 10:16–17).

Many of you have probably fallen on your knees before God and pleaded, "Lord, forgive me of my sin." If that was all God did, it would be wonderful, but Jesus did not come only to forgive us of our sins. He also came to shed His blood in seven places on the mercy seat of God and to break the curse of sin and release us from bondage.

> *Then [the LORD] adds, "Their sins and their lawless deeds I will remember no more." Now where there is remission of these, there is no longer an offering for sin. Therefore, brethren, having boldness to enter the Holiest by the blood of Jesus, by a new and living way which He consecrated for us, through the veil, that is, His flesh, and having a High Priest over the house of God, let us draw near with a true heart in full assurance of faith, having our hearts sprinkled from an evil conscience and our bodies washed with pure water. Let us hold fast the confession of our hope without wavering, for He who promised is faithful. And let us consider one another in order to stir up love and good works.*
> (Hebrews 10:17–24)

One of the names for Yom Kippur in Hebrew literally means "face-to-face." In Exodus, God said to Moses that no man could see Him face-to-face and live. (See Exodus 33:20.) One day a year, however, the high priest was allowed to go before God's presence and talk to Him for the people. Because of Jesus, our onetime blood sacrifice, you and I can now come boldly into the God's presence and meet with Him, personally. This meeting, however, is a gift, not a guarantee.

Because of Jesus, our onetime blood sacrifice, we can now boldly come into God's presence.

Though I speak with the tongues of men and of angels, but have not love, I have become sounding brass or a clanging cymbal. And though I have the gift of prophecy, and understand all mysteries and all knowledge, and though I have all faith, so that I could remove mountains, but have not love, I am nothing. (1 Corinthians 13:1–2)

I may be able to quote the promises and prophecies of Scripture, but if I am also a mean, nasty, racist bigot, then all I'm doing is making sound. I'm nothing more than *"sounding brass or a clanging cymbal."* I may be able to preach golden messages, play an instrument with great skill, or make gobs of money on Wall Street, but if I'm not being the light of the world and the salt of the earth, if I'm not full of love and compassion for other people, then God says I am nothing.

Love never fails. But whether there are prophecies, they will fail; whether there are tongues, they will cease; whether there is knowledge, it will vanish away. For we know in part and we prophesy in part. But when that which is perfect has come, then that which is in part will be done away. When I was a child, I spoke as a child, I understood as a child, I thought as a child; but when I became a man, I put away childish things. For now we see in a mirror, dimly, but then face to face. Now I know in part, but then I shall know just as I also am known. And now abide faith, hope, love, these three; but the greatest of these is love. (1 Corinthians 13:8–13)

The Scapegoat

The sacrificial goat dies so we might live. It is blemished with the blood and the curse of our sin. The high priest emerges from the Holy of Holies, and for all of the following year, the people's sins are covered and God's blessings are released. He dips his hands back into that blood. He confesses the curses. "Father, there are sicknesses, marriages being destroyed, crops failing, animals dying, and wells drying up in this draught." That is the curse of the sin. The sins are covered, but he doesn't just have one sacrifice—he has two.

The sacrificial goat is dead, but what about the other goat? This is the "scapegoat." According to Jewish custom, this is the goat that carries our sins into the desert, never to be remembered. Often, this goat would run off a cliff. If you were to go to Israel, you would see that there is a cliff right beyond the door through which the goat would run. If that goat died, the curses would be broken.

If it survived, it would usually run into the desert. If that goat died in the wilderness, the curses were broken. There is no water in the desert through Jordan to the Red Sea, so the goat would try to get back to the place where it last ate and drank. If the goat managed to come back, the sins of the people remained forgiven, but the curse would remain to block God's blessings.

Jewish lore states that Aaron would tie a red ribbon around the neck of the scapegoat and then attach a portion of the same ribbon to the door of the temple. Every day, they would wait to hear if the goat was dead. If the Jews had repented, and the goat had died in the wilderness, the ribbon on the temple door would miraculously turn white—a visible sign for the people of God's forgiveness. In the Mishna—the books of Jewish wisdom—it is said that sometimes it would turn white and sometimes it would not. Sometimes the curse was broken, and sometimes it was not. The Mishna also states that forty years before the destruction of the temple, the ribbon stopped turning white. Since the temple was destroyed around A.D. 70, the ribbon would have stopped turning white around A.D. 30, or the exact time that Jesus died on the cross, becoming our Passover Lamb and breaking the curse off everyone forever and ever.

Yom Kippur

Primarily, Yom Kippur is a day of repentance. When we repent, it is more than simply confession. One of the Hebrew words for *repent* is *teshuvah*, which means "to return." Repentance, therefore, is more than merely saying you are sorry. It means you will turn away from your sinful path and return to God. It means you aren't going to do it again. Do you have a bad temper? Repent. Are you crabby toward your neighbors or coworkers? Repent. Are you cheating God? Repent. Are you

> Repentance is more than saying you are sorry. It means you will turn away from your sinful path and return to God.

being selfish? Repent. We do so, not to get our tickets punched for heaven, for we are saved by grace, but to have those sins removed so we might be *"white as snow"* (Isaiah 1:18), enter the Holy of Holies, and meet with God, where our names are written in the Book of Blessing.

The second thing we do is fast—go without food—for twenty-four hours. I don't know about you, but I hate fasting. It reminds me of how weak I am and how greatly I am influenced by my physical appetites. When you fast, you are supposed to read your Bible and pray. When I am fasting, it seems like everything I read in the Bible reminds me of food. *"I am the bread of life"* (John 6:48). Oh, the bread of life! *"I have meat to eat ye know not of"* (John 4:32 KJV). Oh, if I could just have a sandwich with meat and bread. That's why, whenever you undertake a fast, it is important to know why you are fasting. In the book of Isaiah, God tells the people they are fasting in the wrong ways and for the wrong reasons.

> *Is this not the fast that I have chosen: to loose the bonds of wickedness, to undo the heavy burdens, to let the oppressed go free, and that you break every yoke? Is it not to share your bread with the hungry, and that you bring to your house the poor who are cast out; when you see the naked, that you cover him, and not hide yourself from your own flesh?*
>
> (Isaiah 58:6–7)

There is something about fasting that awakens your senses to new experiences. When we are fat and stuffed, there are feelings and sensations we miss. When you fast, you do not always feel good. In many ways, fasting reminds us of how others feel. You are hungry. World relief statistics report that one-third of the world goes to bed hungry every night. It's not just people in the third world, though. I don't care where you live, there are people in your community who are hungry. One of the things the church is supposed to do is take care of them. Jesus said, *"For I was hungry and you gave Me food; I was thirsty and you gave Me drink"* (Matthew 25:35). Fasting helps us remember.

> *Then your light shall break forth like the morning, Your healing shall spring forth speedily, and your righteousness shall go before you; the glory of the LORD shall be your rear guard. Then you shall call, and the LORD will answer; you shall cry, and He will say, "Here I am." If*

you take away the yoke from your midst, the pointing of the finger, and speaking wickedness, if you extend your soul to the hungry and satisfy the afflicted soul, then your light shall dawn in the darkness, and your darkness shall be as the noonday. The LORD will guide you continually, and satisfy your soul in drought, and strengthen your bones; you shall be like a watered garden, and like a spring of water, whose waters do not fail. Those from among you shall build the old waste places; You shall raise up the foundations of many generations; and you shall be called the Repairer of the Breach, the Restorer of Streets to Dwell In.

(Isaiah 58:8–12)

Here, God is talking about a year of blessing. First, we repent. Second, we fast for twenty-four hours. We deny ourselves. Just as with Sabbath and Passover, we are not legalistic. Drink water, or perhaps some fruit juice. Do whatever you can to deny yourself. Some people use their hunger pangs as reminders to pray. Believe me, start doing that, and the evil one will stop sending you hunger pangs. Take the money you would have spent on food and give it to charity.

The third thing we do is bring a sacrifice. The word *sacrifice* is not what we have been taught in Christianity. It means "to bring a gift." We think that *sacrifice* means "going without." It doesn't. To *sacrifice* is to bring a gift of honor. We are honoring God for this last year, but we are also honoring God for the year we know He is going to bring us. In Hebrew, *sacrifice* is the word *korban*, whose root word means "nearness" or "close."

In Malachi, God urged His people to return (repent) and draw near (sacrifice) to Him:

"Yet from the days of your fathers you have gone away from My ordinances and have not kept them. Return to Me, and I will return to you," says the LORD of hosts. "But you said, 'In what way shall we return?' Will a man rob God? Yet you have robbed Me! But you say, 'In what way have we robbed You?' In tithes and offerings....Bring all the tithes into the storehouse, that there may be food in My house, and try Me now in this," says the LORD of hosts, "If I will not open for you the windows of heaven and pour out for you such blessing that there will not be room enough to receive it." (Malachi 3:7–8, 10)

God says, "Draw close. I am about to open up the Holy of Holies. I am about to open up the windows of heaven." On Rosh Hashanah, the windows of heaven open; on Yom Kippur, they close. Whoever is in, is in. Whoever is out, is out.

Do you remember when Jesus saw the widow drop her mite into the collection box?

> *Now Jesus sat opposite the treasury and saw how the people put money into the treasury. And many who were rich put in much. Then one poor widow came and threw in two mites, which make a quadrans. So He called His disciples to Himself and said to them, "Assuredly, I say to you that this poor widow has put in more than all those who have given to the treasury; for they all put in out of their abundance, but she out of her poverty put in all that she had, her whole livelihood."*
>
> (Mark 12:41–44)

The widow put everything she had in the hands of God because He was the Source of blessing for the coming year. She wasn't going to need that mite anymore. God says, "Test Me on this one. See if you don't receive more blessing than you can handle."

You may say, "Well, Jesus did not talk about tithing." Actually, He did. Jesus said, *"Woe to you Pharisees! For you tithe mint and rue and all manner of herbs, and pass by justice and the love of God. These you ought to have done, without leaving the others undone"* (Luke 11:42). He commended the Pharisees for tithing, which was a base expectation. Then, He challenged them to do more. Jesus didn't need to talk more on tithing because they were doing it. If you want God to open up windows of heaven, this is the day to make sure that you get on the path so that God can go into the Holy of Holies for you. Jesus paid the price and opened that door, so you and I are no longer separated from God. We can enter in and go before the God of Abraham, Isaac, and Jacob.

What I want, more than anything, is for you to have a firm grasp on who you are in Jesus. *You are a joint heir with Christ!*

You say, "Well, I just got saved." It doesn't matter. You are a joint heir with Christ.

You say, "Well, I used to be a pastor, but I backslid." It doesn't matter. Come back to the Lord; you are a joint heir with Christ.

You say, "Well, I'm a drug dealer and addict, but I'm ready to stop." Turn to God, and you will become a joint heir with Christ Jesus.

Do you know what that means? Do you realize the privilege that you have? As heirs, you can go before your Daddy's throne, just as my grandchildren can rush into my office. Everything will stop.

Just tell Him what you want.

"Jesus, heal me."

It is finished.

"Jesus, bless me."

It is finished.

"Jesus, save my marriage."

It is finished.

"Jesus, save my loved one."

It is finished.

Turn back to Him. Repent, and break the curse.

A Curse Is Broken

Charlotte found herself at a major crisis point in her life. Her husband had suddenly left her. He was a good man, but he had allowed the enemy to plant a seed of division into their marriage. One night, Charlotte woke up crying and turned on the television. Who was on the screen but me, preaching about generational curses, generational blessings, and the Jewish roots of our faith? Charlotte was so moved that she immediately made airline reservations for Dallas so she could attend our next Sunday service. We personally prayed for Charlotte that Sunday and asked that the curse of divorce on her family be broken.

Just after returning to her home in Alabama, Charlotte received a phone call. It was her husband asking if he could see her.

Immediately after walking through the door, he got down on one knee and held out her wedding ring. He asked her to forgive him, accept him back into her life, and remarry him. Charlotte said yes. They have been living "happily ever after" for over two years since. They also have become loyal partners with our ministry and have fallen back in love with each other and with the teaching on Jewish roots.

13

The Feast of Sukkot (Tabernacles)

fter we reflect on our lives and welcome in the fresh start of a new year on Rosh Hashanah, and after we fast and turn back to God in repentance on Yom Kippur, we then come to a season that is called Sukkot, or the Feast of Tabernacles. This is a celebration of the goodness and the joy of the Lord. We have come through a solemn period of reflection and critical self-evaluation. We may not have liked some of the things we saw in ourselves. Thus, we turned back to God to be cleansed in His holiness. Now is a time to celebrate the fact that we survived. We thank God for last year's bountiful harvest and look forward to an even greater harvest blessing of joy, finances, health, family, and ministry.

> *Then the* LORD *spoke to Moses, saying, "Speak to the children of Israel, saying: 'The fifteenth day of this seventh month shall be the Feast of Tabernacles for seven days to the* LORD*....You shall dwell in booths for seven days. All who are native Israelites shall dwell in booths, that your generations may know that I made the children of Israel dwell in booths when I brought them out of the land of Egypt: I am the* LORD *your God.'" So Moses declared to the children of Israel the feasts of the* LORD. (Leviticus 23:33–34, 42–44)

The Feast of Tabernacles, or Sukkot, is very similar to what we in America celebrate at Thanksgiving. It occurs at almost the same time of year. In fact, according to historians, the pilgrims actually had the first Thanksgiving on and possibly directly inspired by Sukkot. The pilgrims were very religious people. When they came out of Europe, they saw it as symbolic of Israel coming out of Egypt. To these early settlers, God bringing them across the Atlantic Ocean to their Promised Land was akin to the Israelites passing through the Red Sea. The reason they came was to worship the God of Abraham, Isaac, and Jacob, free from the persecution of the Catholic Church and the Church of England. They called themselves Judeo-Christians. After they arrived, they experienced many hardships, but they also recognized the blessings God provided for them.

God's Miracle Provision

Today, we are so familiar with the deliverance story of Israel from Egypt that the details can almost seem mundane. But when you think about it, Israel really should have perished many times during this story. Consider all of the unlikely events. First, the murderous and power-hungry pharaoh let them go. Second, they left with all the wealth of Egypt. Third, with Pharaoh's chariots in hot pursuit, God parted an ocean for them to escape. Fourth, with little food and water in the hot desert, God provided manna every day and made water flow from a rock. They experienced no sickness. Their shoes never wore out.

> God is *Jehovah Jireh*, the One who heals and the One who delivers.

To commemorate this miraculous time, God asked His people to construct "booths" to serve as a reminder of their temporary dwellings when they passed through the wilderness. It was to remind them that God is *Jehovah Jireh*, the One who heals and the One who delivers. He is the One who destroys our enemies and provides food and water in the dry places. Why is it so important to have these reminders? Once again, God is painfully aware of our short memories.

When you have eaten and are full, and have built beautiful houses and dwell in them; and when your herds and your flocks multiply, and your silver and your gold are multiplied, and all that you have is multiplied; when your heart is lifted up, and you forget the LORD your God who brought you out of the land of Egypt, from the house of bondage; who led you through that great and terrible wilderness, in which were fiery serpents and scorpions and thirsty land where there was no water; who brought water for you out of the flinty rock; who fed you in the wilderness with manna, which your fathers did not know, that He might humble you and that He might test you, to do you good in the end; then you say in your heart, "My power and the might of my hand have gained me this wealth." And you shall remember the LORD *your God, for it is He who gives you power to get wealth, that He may establish His covenant which He swore to your fathers, as it is this day.*

(Deuteronomy 8:12–18)

So, every year, God told His people to build a small tabernacle and to dwell in it for seven days. When Israel was wandering in the wilderness for forty years, they would build themselves shelters that they could immediately take down, wrap up, and put away. These were made mostly out of poles and animal pelts and palm leaves—whatever they could find. They had to be portable and lightweight because the people had to be constantly ready for God's newest instructions. They had to be able to see through the tops because God was leading them with a pillar of cloud by day and a pillar of fire by night. These signs were their GPS system, and they had to be able to see them constantly in case they began to move. If they lost track of the pillars, and therefore of God, they knew that the desert they were in would eventually devour them. What does this say to us today? No matter how blessed we are, we have to keep our eyes on God, because He is our Covering, our Provider, and our Healer. If we lose sight of Him, the world we're in may destroy us, as well.

If you've ever been to Israel, you know that the desert is not just warm, it's lethally hot. That's why the pillar during the day was a cloud, which shaded them. At nighttime, the desert can actually be a very cold place. Therefore, the pillar at night was made of fire, which warmed them. They may have been wandering the wilderness, but they were also wandering in the supernatural. It was supernatural that they came out with all of Egypt's silver and gold. It was supernatural that they walked across a parted sea only to watch it "unpart" and destroy their enemies. It was supernatural for water to come out of a rock. It was supernatural for food to fall from the sky. It was supernatural that, after walking in the desert for forty years, their shoes and clothing never wore out or rotted. It was supernatural that no one ever got sick. But then God said, "You ain't seen nothing yet. This next year, I've got more blessings for you than you've ever imagined. But don't take your eyes off Me, because I am the One who brings you covering during the day and protection at night. If you take your eyes off Me and put them on what you have, or if you're not willing to move when I say to move, then the anointing will leave you, and you'll be alone in the wilderness."

When we're most in need, we keep our eyes on God. We pray diligently, "Oh, God, help me!" Then, after the answer comes, we become a little lukewarm. When our marriages are healed and our careers have taken off, we can begin to lose sight of the Lord. So, God wants to remind us that in the wilderness, it was supernatural. For forty years, the Israelites had to depend on a supernatural God. There were no stores, no crops, and no water. For forty years, there was just Jehovah Jireh, who was more than enough.

Feast of Nations

Sukkot is also called the Feast of Nations. On this day, God asked the Israelites to sacrifice seventy bulls. That may seem strange in today's world, but, the Bible claims that there were seventy nations at the time. In Hebrew, the word *salvation* is the word *sozo*, which means "forgiveness," but it also means "prosperity," "healing," "joy," "happiness," and "peace." What they were doing was making a sacrifice not just for the Jewish people but also for every nation on earth. Remember, God told Abraham that through him, all nations would be blessed.

In Jewish teaching, there is what is called the Messianic period, a time when the Messiah will come, and all the nations on earth will recognize Him and gather on Sukkot at Jerusalem, where we will live under the blessing of the Messiah, and every area of our lives will be taken care of forever. Thus, beginning on Sukkot and going for seven days, all the priests in Jerusalem would gather together at the temple and divide into three different groups. One group would go out the main gate. Another group would go out the east gate. The third group would go out the water gate. One group would go out to gather the sacrifices for a blood offering. The next group would go down to a certain area off to the west of Jerusalem, where they would cut long branches off of willow trees. The third group would go with the high priest to the pool of Shalom—the same pool where Jesus healed the blind man—and use a golden pitcher to gather its "living water." Accompanying them would be an assistant carrying a pitcher of wine.

At a certain moment, all three groups would head toward the gates of the temple. The shofar would blow, and the three groups would meet at exactly the same moment with the sacrifice, the trees, and the water and wine. At the moment they all met, the shofar was blown again. This would call forth a man who would begin to play a flute—always a symbol of the coming Messiah, who was also called "the pierced one." The first group would be the ones with the bulls—a sacrifice so all the world could be adopted into the family of the God of Abraham, Isaac, and Jacob. After the blood was all over the altar, they would remove the carcasses. Then would come the ones with the trees, and they would arrange the trees over the altar, angling them upward to make a tabernacle or a wedding canopy. Thus, the blood is shed and the canopy is built, symbolizing that the Messiah would come and be the Bridegroom for all of God's people. The third priest would then come and pour the water onto that blood, symbolizing the Holy Spirit and an outpouring of joy. Then, the associate priest would pour wine onto the water and the blood, the symbol of a marriage covenant. Imagine how powerful it was for first-century Jews who were familiar with this ceremony when Jesus went to a wedding feast in Cana and turned water into fine wine. What better way could there have been for Jesus to announce that the Messiah had come?

Call Forth the Messiah

Now let's fast-forward to the first century. It is the Feast of Tabernacles, and Jesus is in the temple celebrating Sukkot.

> Now the Jews' Feast of Tabernacles was at hand....On the last day, that great day of the feast, Jesus stood and cried out, saying, "If anyone thirsts, let him come to Me and drink. He who believes in Me, as the Scripture has said, out of his heart will flow rivers of living water."
> (John 7:2, 37–38)

Now, unless you are familiar with the Jewish roots of your faith, how can you know what this passage really means? This was the final day of the feast—the day on which all the people got to come into the temple. On the seventh day, the priest would pour water on the altar seven times, and they would all walk around that altar seven times, each time shouting, "Save us!" They were calling for their Messiah.

Jesus stood up at the Sukkot celebration and said, "I'm here! I've come to give you living water. When you taste Me, you'll never thirst again." What an amazing event. Jesus was right there with them. He watched them walk around the altar. He watched them pour "living water" on the altar. They started calling for the Messiah to come and bring His kingdom on earth, and He said, "Here I am!"

Ingathering

Sukkot is also called the Feast of Ingathering. Today, Jews all over the world keep Sukkot by building small booths outside in their yards, and the doors are never closed. At all other times, God's people live behind closed doors and invite people over for dinner and fellowship. Others are welcome, but they must be invited because the doors are closed. On Sukkot, the Feast of Tabernacles, the Feast of Ingathering, the doors remain open. All Jews know that if you see a tabernacle, you can go in there as a stranger, but you will walk out as a family member.

If you have loved ones who are not born again, you need to claim this month for their salvation.

What does this mean to us? If you have loved ones who are not born again, you need to claim this month for their salvation. Jesus said, *"I am the door. If anyone enters by Me, he will be saved"* (John 10:9). Jesus is the door, and it's open to everybody!

Sukkot is also a time for you to gather your harvest—not only saved souls, but also your financial harvest. Say these words: "He has opened the door, I'm keeping my eyes on Him, and I'm going to have the best year of my life so far."

14

Your Exciting Journey!

My greatest desire in writing this book is to connect people with the God of Abraham, Isaac, and Jacob. My goal in all that I study and teach is to connect the dots of faith and to create a path of learning, revelation, and enlightenment. As the Lord reveals His mysteries to me, and as I convey them to you, I pray that the miracles of the Bible will be released into your lives—just as they have been released in my life!

This journey has brought such incredible joy, hunger, and excitement into my life and the lives of my family. It really has been, and continues to be, a never-ending story. Each new revelation leads to the discovery of the next. These new revelations are actually not new at all, but are, in fact, as old as time. We are finally returning to the foundations that the Lord intended for us to live by and build upon all along.

God's Word has never been solely for the purpose of recording the history of what He did for His people in the past. It is also to show us what He intends and desires to do for His people now and in the future! These incredible teachings, traditions, and foundations are not to be cast away and forgotten as ancient ruins but are to be preserved and built upon in our lives and in the generations to come! In his book, *This Is My God*, Herman Wouk stated, "I believe it is our lot to live and to serve in our old identity, until the promised day when the Lord will be one and His name one in all the earth. I think the extinction of Jewish learning and Jewish faith would be a measureless tragedy." I absolutely and wholeheartedly agree.

I'm sure that this book will stir up controversy from both Christian and Jewish circles. Attempting to tear down the barriers and walls between Judaism and Christianity is certainly bound to spark age-old, highly opinionated, and emotionally-charged viewpoints. My goal is to provoke a new way of thinking that will produce a new wave of results.

I know that this book will probably raise more questions than it answers. One of the biggest challenges in writing it has been to condense all that I have studied, read, and learned over the past decade into a relatively short text. To do so requires that that I attempt to summarize subjects that have spanned nearly all of history, filled thousand of libraries, and been at the center of world controversies and on-going wars! Along the way, however, I have discovered that many people are extremely curious about these subjects just as I am, but they have no idea where to start on this incredibly vast journey. So, I would ask my readers, including any skeptics or critics, to view this book not as an exhaustive, all-inclusive work with all the answers to every question, but as a beginning, a starting point, a place to begin a journey. It is a journey of exciting and illuminating discovery into the heart and the Word of our God.

Thirty-four years ago, I had an encounter with the Lord that changed me forever. The power of God transformed me from an angry young man who was lost, confused, and bound by drugs and alcohol into a man of God. Thirteen years ago, I had an encounter with the Lord that was equally life changing. As I confessed on the first page of the introduction to this book, as a pastor, I was becoming disillusioned and weary. I was not seeing the manifestation of the promises in the Word of God to the degree that I desired. Something was missing. When I discovered the 2000-year-old missing puzzle piece, my life was, once again, changed forever! A light went on within me. A fire was ignited that has been burning every day since! My hunger for God and for His Word has become insatiable! Never in my thirty-four years as a Christian, or as a pastor, have I been so excited about learning and teaching the truths of the Bible! And never have I seen so many miracles manifested or prayers answered, both in my own life and in the lives of those who are grasping these truths!

That is why I pray that you, too, become "infected" with this contagious enthusiasm and appetite. There is an old saying that says, "Truths are not so much taught as they are caught." I hope that you are able to understand the things in this book that I have taught. But, even more, I hope that you have caught the heart and soul of these truths and that they will bring as much blessing to you and your family as they have to mine.

When Jesus came the first time, His mission was to bring people back into a right relationship with God the Father, and to bring the world back to a correct understanding and following of the Word of God. He was bringing people back to the Torah. He tried to disassociate the people from man-made religious traditions that were, for the most part, lifeless and burdensome. His teachings and His lifestyle brought people back into a personal, vibrant, and fresh relationship with God Himself. The anointing on His life released the supernatural power of God into the lives of everyone He touched. As Jesus revealed the mysteries, the miracles were released.

I believe that this will be his same mission in His Second Coming. We live in a time when it's fashionable to be a non-believer. There has never been a time when there has been greater skepticism and cynicism about religion. And yet, there has never been a greater need or hunger for meaning and purpose. In our current world, filled with chaos and uncertainty, there is a great vacuum of hope, direction, and answers. People have been searching for wisdom and love in all the wrong places. They have exhausted every avenue. This is the perfect arena for the Messiah to come!

This is also the perfect time to come back to the Word of God, to the traditions of the Torah, and to the time-tested truths that are the foundations for a wonderful life and world! As the Bible teaches, *"You shall know the truth, and the truth shall make you free"* (John 8:32). As that day quickly approaches, the Bible promises that masses of peoples' hearts will turn to God. There will be a great outpouring of signs, wonders, and miracles! The clock is ticking and the Lord is raising up His people of miracles! We need to get ready and get positioned for all that the Lord is going to do within us, for us, and through us! It is time to reveal the mysteries and release the miracles!

May the God of Abraham, Isaac, and Jacob bless you on your exciting journey!

Shabbat Shalom!

Appendix:
The Seven Major Jewish Feasts

Feast	Jewish Tradition / Christian Parallels	Bible Ref.	Dates	Ways to Celebrate
Feast of Unleavened Bread	A week of eating bread made without yeast (matzah) to remember how God brought the Israelites out of Egypt in haste. For Christians, remembering that Jesus is the Bread of Life and our Sustainer.	Leviticus 23:4,6–8	(Seven day period.) Sundown 3/29–4/6/2010 4/18–26/2011 4/6–14/2012 3/25–4/2/2013	Clear your house of leavened bread and eat only matzah for seven days as a rejection of sin in your life. (pp. 145–146)
Feast of Passover (*Pesach*)	Remembering the Exodus from Egypt and God's deliverance of the Jews from centuries of slavery. Preparation for their entry into the Promised Land. For Christians, a reminder that we were once lost, but now are saved.	Leviticus 23:4–8 Exodus 12	(First two nights of Feast of Unleavened Bread.) Sundown 3/29–31/2010 4/18–20/2011 4/6–8/2012 3/25–27/2013	Celebrate a Seder dinner with family and friends. (pp. 146–168)
Feast of First Fruits	Presenting a sheaf of the first fruits of the harvest. For Christians, a reminder that everything we have comes from God.	Leviticus 23:10–14	(Day after Sabbath during Passover.) Sundown 4/3/2010 4/23/2011 4/7/2012 3/30/2013	Make an extra offering—above your tithe—in thankfulness for your next year of blessing. (pp. 168–170)

Feast	Jewish Tradition / Christian Parallels	Bible Ref.	Dates	Ways to Celebrate
Feast of Pentecost (*Shavuot*)	A release of God's double blessing. (A Sabbath of Sabbaths.) Celebrates the Lord giving the Law to Moses on Mount Sinai. For Christians a celebration of when the Holy Spirit first fell upon Jesus' followers.	Leviticus 23:15–25	(Fifty days after Passover.) Sundown 5/18/2010 6/7/2011 3/26/2012 5/14/2013	Get with church or prayer group and anoint everybody's hands for prosperity. Lay hands on every forehead for wisdom and the gifts of the Holy Spirit. Pray for all curses to be broken and all debts to be cancelled. (pp. 174–176)
Feast of Rosh Hashanah Jewish New Year or Feast of Trumpets	Celebrates the beginning of the Jewish Civil year. It is both a time of rejoicing as well as reflection and self-evaluation. For Christians, a reminder to be prepared for the rapture to come.	Leviticus 23:23–25	(First day of Jewish calendar) Sundown 9/18/2009 9/8/2010 9/28/2011 9/16/2012 9/4/2013	The night we celebrate what God has done, and then, take stock of our lives and turn back to God. (pp. 177–181)
Feast of Yom Kippur Day of Atonement	Holiest day of the Jewish year. High Priest would enter the Holy of Holies to offer a sacrifice for the sins of Israel. For Christians, a time to celebrate Jesus' sacrifice allowing us to personally go before God.	Leviticus 16:1–34 23:26–32	(Ten days after Rosh Hashanah) Sundown 9/27/2009 9/17/2010 10/7/2011 9/25/2012 9/13/2013	Go on a fast for twenty-four hours. Allow it to reveal ways in which you are weak. Bring a sacrifice, or gift, to your house of worship in gratefulness. (pp. 187–199)
Feast of Tabernacles (*Sukkot*) Feast of Ingathering/ Feast of Nations	Recalls forty years of wandering in the wilderness, living in tents, and worshipping in a portable tabernacle. Temporary booths are constructed to remind Israel of the wilderness wandering. For Christians, a reflection of the Second Coming and millennial reign of Jesus on earth.	Leviticus 23:33–43	(Seven days, first day being a Sabbath.) Sundown 10/2–9/2009 9/22–29/2010 10/12–19/2011 9/31–10/7/2012 9/18–25/2013	Claim salvation for unsaved family members and loved ones. Proclaim the blessings that God is going to bestow on you over the next year. Gather with friends, saved and unsaved. (pp. 201–206)

For additional future dates of Jewish feasts and holidays, see the Web site: www.Chabad.org.

Glossary of Terms

Afikomen
: Greek, meaning "dessert." Half of the middle matzah, which, when broken off, is placed back with the others until the end of the meal.

Arba kanfot
: Hebrew for "four wings"—or corners—of a Jewish tallit.

Challah
: Traditional, braided Jewish bread used in Sabbath celebrations.

Charoset
: An ingredient in the Seder meal, a mixture made from apples or dates, nuts, honey, and cinnamon, representing the mortar Jewish slaves used to make bricks for Egypt.

Ethnos
: Greek word for Gentiles.

Gentile
: Any non-Jewish person.

Haggadah
: The order of service and text for the Seder celebration.

Kiddush
: A blessing recited over wine or grape juice to sanctify the Sabbath or Jewish holidays.

Kraspedon
: Hebrew for "hem," used to refer to the hem of Jesus' garment and thought to be the twisted wool tassels of a tallit.

Logos
: Greek word for "the written word," also used for "logic."

Maror
: Derives from Hebrew word for "bitter"; traditionally, a piece of raw horseradish root is symbolically placed on the Seder plate.

Menuhah	Hebrew word for "rest," as found in Genesis 2:2, "*He rested on the seventh day.*" Not meaning "sleep," but rather "peace," "harmony," "happiness," or "no strife."
Mezuzah	A small plaque or parchment applied to the doorway of every Jewish home and containing words from the Shema. Fulfills a mitzvah from God in Deuteronomy 6:9.
Midrash	Written homilies and studies and interpretations of Old Testament Scripture.
Mishna	Written form of Jewish oral traditions, also called the oral Torah.
Mitzvah	Hebrew for "commandment." Refers to the commandments given to us by God. Not just the Ten Commandments, however, but all 613 mitzvahs found in Scripture.
Nomos	Greek word for "law," usually as it is enforced by religious institutions. A way to be accepted or acceptable.
Passover	In Hebrew, *Pesach*, a yearly Jewish feast, or holy day, recalling Israel's exodus from Egypt and deliverance from slavery. Literally refers to the plague God sent Pharaoh that killed all the first born sons of Egypt. The Jew's application of lamb's blood on their doorpost cause the curse to "pass over" their household.
Pesach	(See Passover.)
Rabbi	Hebrew word meaning "great" or "revered," usually referring to a Jewish man who was a teacher of the Torah. Not an occupation but a title.
Rhema	Greek term for the Word of God made alive by the inspiration of the Holy Spirit.
Rosh Hashanah	Hebrew for "head of the year." First day of the Jewish calendar and a ten day period of reflection and repentance leading to Yom Kippur, the Day of Atonement.

Sabbath	Shabbat in Hebrew, a day of rest, beginning at sundown every Friday.
Seder	Hebrew word for "order" or "arrangement," but also referring to the meal and ceremony on the first and second night of Passover.
Shabbat	Hebrew word for Sabbath meaning "rest" or "to cease." (See Sabbath.)
Shalom	Hebrew for "peace" in the sense of wholeness, completeness, and welfare. Also a Hebrew blessing for "hello" and "goodbye."
Shavuot	Hebrew for "weeks." Denotes the Feast of Pentecost, celebrating when God gave Moses the first five books of the Old Testament on Mount Sinai.
Shema	Hebrew word for "hear." First word of the daily Jewish prayer that says, "Hear, O Israel: the Lord is our God, the Lord is One." (See Deuteronomy 6:4.)
Shofar	Ancient trumpet made from a horn. Blown in preparation for Rosh Hashanah and Yom Kippur.
Sukkot	Hebrew word, plural for "booth" or "hut." Signifies the Feast of Tabernacles, celebrated for seven days after Yom Kippur. A reminder of when Israel lived in the wilderness in makeshift tents, and later worshipped in a portable tabernacle, a forerunner to a permanent temple.
Tallit	A prayer shawl traditionally worn as an outer garment by Jewish men. Edge of the tallit has tassels made with blue thread at the four corners, or wings.
Torah	Hebrew word for "learning," "instruction," or "law." God's Word or law as a pathway to relationship with our Father. Also refers to the first five books of the Old Testament.
Tzedakah	Hebrew word commonly translated as "charity," but also part of the root word of "justice." Used to refer to acts of kindness.

Tzedakah Box   A small receptacle in which Jewish children save their money for use in acts of charity.

Yarmulke   Also *kippah,* or skull cap, worn by Jewish men in synagogue or on holy days.

Yeshua   Common name during the Second Temple Period in Jewish history. Believed to be the Hebrew or Aramaic equivalent of the English name Jesus.

Yom Kippur   Hebrew for the Day of Atonement. The most solemn of Jewish holidays. During temple worship, it was the day the high priest went into the Holy of Holies to offer a sacrifice that would forgive the sins of the nation for another year.

Zakar   Hebrew word for "mark," used in the commandment to remember the Sabbath and keep it holy.

About Larry Huch

L arry Huch is the founder and senior pastor of DFW New Beginnings in Irving, Texas. Founded in November 2004, this nondenominational church has quickly developed into a diverse, multiethnic congregation of several thousand people. Pastor Larry and his wife, Tiz, are driven by a passionate commitment to see people succeed in every area of life. That passion, along with their enthusiasm, genuine love for people, and effective teaching, has fueled a ministry that spans over thirty years and two continents.

That same energy and commitment to sharing a positive, life-changing, and biblically based message with the world is the hallmark of Pastor Larry's international television program, *New Beginnings*. This program is broadcast weekly to millions of homes around the globe and has served to touch and change the lives of countless people.

Pastor Larry's signature combination of humor, a dynamic teaching style, and a deep understanding of the Bible have made him a much sought after guest on television programs, conferences, and various other forms of media. Pastor Larry is a pioneer in the area of breaking family curses and has been recognized the world over for his teachings on the subject, along with his best-selling book, *Free at Last*. His successful follow-up book, *10 Curses That Block the Blessing*, is also a best seller. As a successful author, Pastor Larry has been honored by the testimonies of thousands upon thousands of people whose lives have been impacted and forever altered by his testimony and teachings.

Pastor Larry is wholeheartedly committed to bridging the gap between Christians and Jews and restoring the church to its Judeo-Christian roots. He firmly believes in studying, understanding, and teaching the Word from a Jewish perspective. Larry was honored to have spoken at the Israeli Knesset and has received awards from the Knesset Social Welfare Lobby for his ministry's generosity toward the needs of the Jewish people in Israel.

Pastors Larry and Tiz are the proud parents of three wonderful children (and a son-in-law and daughter-in-law), all who are active in ministry. Their three grandchildren, the "Sugars," are the loves of their lives!

No Limits, No Boundaries:
Praying Dynamic Change into Your Life, Family, & Finances
Tiz Huch

Through prayer, we can see the promises that are written in the Word manifest as realities in our lives. Tiz Huch has a deep passion to teach people how to pray with the power to achieve specific results. *No Limits, No Boundaries* will take your prayer life to a whole new level, infusing you with God's strength, confidence, and boldness to walk in the dominion and authority that God Himself has intended for you.

ISBN: 978-1-60374-119-4 • Trade • 240 pages

WHITAKER
HOUSE

10 Curses That Block the Blessing
Larry Huch

Have you been suffering with depression, family dysfunction, marital unhappiness, or other problems and been unable to overcome them? Within the pages of this groundbreaking book, *10 Curses That Block the Blessing*, Larry Huch shares his personal experience with a life of anger, drug addiction, crime, and violence. He shows how he broke these curses and reveals how you can recognize the signs of a curse, be set free from generational curses, and restore your health and wealth. You don't have to struggle any longer. Choose to revolutionize your life. You can reverse the curses that block your blessings!

ISBN: 978-0-88368-207-4 ✦ Trade ✦ 224 pages

WHITAKER
HOUSE

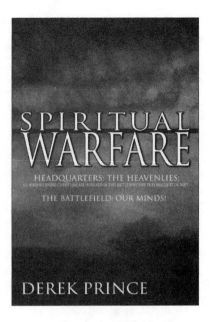

Spiritual Warfare
Derek Prince

Resist the enemy's attacks.
Tear down the enemy's strongholds.
Learn the key to victory.

Derek Prince explains the battle that's happening now
between the forces of God and the forces of evil. Choose
to be prepared by learning the enemy's strategies so you can
effectively block his attacks. We have God on our side, and
nothing will keep us from victory!

ISBN: 978-0-88368-670-6 ♦ Trade ♦ 144 pages

WHITAKER
HOUSE

Lucifer Exposed: The Devil's Plan to Destroy Your Life
Derek Prince

Satan, the fallen archangel, desires nothing more than to win the loyalty, hearts, and minds of the entire human race—and he won't quit in his attempt to win you over! Are you—or someone you know—struggling with abuse, pornography, addiction, gluttony, or other issues? Use the mighty spiritual weapons revealed in this compelling book, and victory can be yours!

ISBN: 978-0-88368-836-6 ◆ Trade ◆ 160 pages

WHITAKER
HOUSE

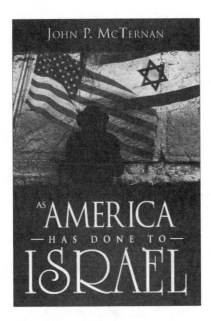

As America Has Done to Israel
John P. McTernan

God's everlasting promise to bless those who bless Israel—
and curse those who curse Israel—is still in effect today.
Throughout its history, America has been in a unique position
to bless the Jewish people and has experienced many blessings
as a result. In more recent years, however, America has failed to
consistently stand by Israel and suffered dramatic disasters. In this
thought-provoking book, John McTernan traces how America's
spectacular rise to power was tied to blessing the Jews. He also
examines the times when America defaulted on this call—and the
dire consequences that followed. Torn from today's headlines, *As
America Has Done to Israel* is a must-read for all Christians who
love God, love their country, and desire to walk in His ways!

ISBN: 978-1-60374-038-8 • Trade • 320 pages

WHITAKER
HOUSE

Free at Last: Removing the Past from Your Future
(with Study Guide CD)
Larry Huch

You can break free from your past! Don't let what has happened to you and your family hold you back in life. You can find freedom from depression, anger, abuse, insecurity, and addiction in Jesus Christ. Pastor Larry Huch reveals powerful truths from Scripture that enabled him and many others to quickly break the destructive chains in their lives and receive God's blessings. Learn the secret to true freedom and you, too, can regain your joy and hope, experience divine health, mend broken relationships, and walk in true prosperity—body, soul, and spirit.

ISBN: 978-0-88368-428-3 • Trade with CD • 272 pages

WHITAKER
HOUSE